THE POWER WITHIN

SOMATIC & SPIRITUAL STORIES OF RESILIENCE

NICOLE SMITH LEVAY

+10 Authors from the Power Within Healing Community

The Power Within: Somatic & Spiritual Stories of Resilience

ISBN: 978-1-962407-99-1 (paperback)
ISBN: 978-1-962407-50-2 (hardcover)
ISBN: 978-1-962407-49-6 (eBook)

Contents

Foreword

The Power Within

Kate Butler, CPSC

If you looked only at where I am today, you might assume it was always easy, that I always believed in myself, that success came naturally. But the truth is, every milestone I've reached began with a struggle I had to overcome.

For much of my life, I carried a heavy weight that whispered: *You're not enough.*

Growing up, I never felt "enough." I wrestled with learning challenges, battled with severe depression and became my own worst enemy through devastating self-sabotage. Each setback reinforced the story in my head that I was unworthy, that I didn't have what it took to succeed, and that my voice didn't matter. For years, I carried that belief, letting it dictate what I thought was possible.

It wasn't until I began doing the work to heal within, quieting the self-doubt, untangling the stories I told myself, and beginning to believe I was whole and worthy, that things started to shift. Healing gave me the courage to write my first book, to say yes to my story, and eventually to guide others to share theirs.

But here's what I've learned: no external accomplishment can ever make you feel worthy. Worthiness is not given, it is something you claim. It wasn't until I turned inward, faced the delicate places of doubt, and began the deep work of healing that I finally discovered the truth: I had always been whole. I had always been worthy. I simply needed to remember it.

That shift changed everything.

Once I stopped seeking permission outside of myself and started living from a place of wholeness, doors I never imagined possible began to open. The very girl who once failed English class went on to become a 25-time #1 International Best-Selling Author. Each book I've written has been both a mirror and a message, reminding me, and others, of the power of owning our voice. I also had the honor of publishing over 700 best-selling authors, guiding hundreds of others to share their stories and turn their words into movements that ripple out into the world. I eventually went on to build a multi–seven-figure business once I fully stepped into my truth: that living on purpose, showing up to help, heal and inspire others through my work and leading with love were the keys to my freedom.

What once felt impossible became my reality, not through hustle alone, but by aligning with purpose, healing my beliefs around worthiness, and daring to step fully into the life I was called to live.

None of this would have been possible without healing. Healing the unworthiness. Healing the self-doubt. Healing the illusion that I wasn't enough.

And that's why *The Power Within* is more than a book, it is an invitation. Within these pages, you'll discover stories of extraordinary courage and resilience. You'll meet people who faced heartbreak, illness, trauma, or loss, and chose not to stay in the shadows but to walk toward light, wholeness, and renewal.

Their stories remind us that healing isn't about fixing what's broken. It's about remembering who we already are: whole, worthy, powerful.

As you read, I hope you find yourself reflected here. I hope you hear the quiet whisper that I once heard, the one that says: You are enough. You are worthy. You are whole. And you are capable of creating the life you desire.

May this book be your companion and your catalyst, a reminder that the power to heal has always been within you.

With so much love for you,

With a
Grateful Heart
– Kate ♡

ABOUT KATE BUTLER, CPSC

Kate Butler is a #1 International Best-selling and Award-winning author and speaker. As a CPSC, Certified Professional Success Coach, she offers clients dynamic programs to help them reach their ultimate potential and live out their dreams. She does this through mindset, success, and book publishing programs. Kate is also the creator of the Inspired Impact Book Series, which has published fifteen titles.

Kate received her double major degree in Mass Communications and Interpersonal Communication Studies from Towson University in Maryland. After ten years in the corporate world, Kate decided it was time to fulfill her true passion; she studied business at Wharton School of Business at The University of Pennsylvania and received her certificate in Entrepreneur Acceleration.

Kate now brings her expertise to mainstream media where she has been featured as the Mindset and Publishing expert on Fox 29, Good Day Philadelphia, HBO, in the Huffington Post, and on various other television, news, and radio platforms.

To learn more about becoming an author in the Inspired Impact Book Series, or to learn how to work with Kate directly on achieving your goals or publishing your book (including children's books), visit her website at www.katebutlerbooks.com. Kate would love to connect with you!

To Connect with Kate:

Facebook: @katebutlerbooks
Instagram: @katebutlerbooks
Website: www.katebutlerbooks.com

Content Considerations & Trigger Warnings

We hope this collection leaves you feeling empowered and inspired, and we also recognize that the path to healing sometimes brings up difficult emotions.

Within these pages, you'll find real peoples' stories through and about mental health, grief, chronic pain, trauma, suicidality, bullying, addiction, death, and loss—experiences often unspoken in everyday life.

Please care for yourself as you move through these essays. Take breaks. Pause when needed. Let the stories unfold one at a time. You are under no obligation to rush or read straight through.

In the end, this book is here to remind you that you are not alone, healing is possible, and that even in the hardest moments, there is still a power within.

This content is for personal development purposes and not intended to be a substitute for professional medical advice, diagnosis, or treatment. Always seek the advice of your physician or other qualified health professional.

Acknowledgements

I want to take a moment to honor and acknowledge every soul who helped bring this book to life.

First, deep gratitude to Kate Butler for the life-changing invitation to create this anthology, and to her entire team for believing in this work and supporting us through every detail. Thank you for seeing the power of these voices.

To each of our contributing authors: thank you for your trust, your courageous vulnerability, and your willingness to share what others might keep hidden. Your stories are bold, necessary, and deeply human. I am endlessly proud of what we've created together.

To our friends, families, and healing community: thank you for encouraging us to write, for nudging us forward when the process got hard, and for holding space as we gave language to pain, joy, and everything in between.

And to my husband, Bill Levay: thank you for being the unwavering support behind every wild idea I chase. You've not only nurtured every word I've written, but also generously volunteered your time to support our authors through their early drafts. You are the quiet glue that holds more than most people know. Everyone loves you, for good reason!

This book was never just about getting words on a page. It was about ensuring our authors felt seen and supported at every level of their writing and healing journey. And now, dear reader, I want the same for you.

With love and reverence,

Nicole

Get Up, Nicole.

Nicole Smith Levay

Every day, I work with women who feel helpless, hopeless, and deeply alone. They are brilliant, strong, talented, and often outwardly successful, but inside they feel exhausted, scared, and out of control. Through transformational retreats at inspiring locations around the world and one-on-one somatic coaching, I help high-achieving women stop over-giving on autopilot and finally put themselves and their purpose work first, using the tools of somatics, breathwork, and meditation.

For over a decade, I've had the privilege of witnessing thousands of women move from burnout to feeling revitalized, from loathing their jobs to resurrecting their purpose, from living in their heads to reconnecting with their bodies and reclaiming their authentic selves from the inside out.

That's why this book was born. Over the years, I began to notice how many of the women I worked with carried stories that mirrored my own. Stories of silence, sensitivity, survival, and resilience. One by one, we began to speak them out loud, and something shifted. This anthology is a preservation of those shifts.

It is a gathering of voices from women who once felt lost in the noise but have found a way back to their truth. Together, we wrote this book for the woman still searching. To remind her that she is not alone. That healing is possible. And that her story, too, is important.

* * *

If you had asked me as a child what I wanted to be when I grew up, I probably would have said an opera singer. There was something majestic about one woman standing alone, unapologetically shaking the room with her sound.

That image felt worlds away from my internal experience. As a ballet dancer, I lived with a constant internal tape loop of self-criticism and judgment. I felt voiceless, frozen, and incapable of withstanding the pressures of life.

I never imagined I would become a helper, healer, or therapist. If anything, I thought my worth came solely from others helping me. I lived in a home where my basic needs were met and I was safe, but I didn't feel loved, and I felt profoundly alone and misunderstood.

I was 16 years old, in the honor society, and had just quit the dance equivalent of child acting (dancing in the second company at the Joffrey Ballet School). I had never experienced the loss of a loved one or serious heartbreak of any kind. Anxiously, I became consumed with applying to colleges, unclear about my next steps, sort of plowing through life at warp speed.

Like a good girl, following what I thought were the rules of the game, I sucked in any sense of self-worth from praise I received to hold me over till the next day. Thinking: one day, "When I achieve XYZ," I would be OK, and then life would actually start. So I just had to get "there," and soon. Then things would get easier.

Perhaps you have also felt that way? But where is *there*?

And when are the achievements and accolades ever enough?

Yet there was a pivotal moment for me that brought me to doing this work myself. My own dark night of the soul that took me to death's door one night in high school and began a healing journey at that young age.

If the hospital hadn't been seven minutes away, I might not be here to share how I went from wanting to end it all to finding the path of deep healing and purpose.

* * *

He was my first love, the most talented, brilliant boy in the drama club. And he chose me? The lanky, flat-chested, anxious girl who secretly believed no one actually liked her. I'd had boyfriends before, but he was the first to make me feel truly seen and heard. He was so smart, so magnetic, and a rogue soul like me, trying to break free from perfectionism and societal molds of the "good kids."

One key difference: I'm white. He was brown. It was the year 2000. Both our families, somewhat surprisingly to us, disapproved of our dating and let us know that privately.

But we were in love, and that was all that mattered, really. We snuck around like high schoolers do. That summer, I felt unconditional love for the first time. We were Romeo and Juliet, for better or for worse.

When he left for college, he promised we'd stay together. About a month later, I visited him at UPenn's prestigious Wharton School. I felt proud. My boyfriend was not only a genius, charismatic, and popular with his friends, he was mine too. That night, things felt a bit different at times, but I brushed it off. We hung out late into the night with his friends, and later, I slept over, and we were intimate in his twin-size dorm room bed.

Then, the next morning, he walked me to the train going back to New Jersey, and there on the station platform, like some bad romance movie, I noticed his energy shifted drastically. Eyes lowered, nervous and tense, he told me he had to tell me something.

"Ok, you can tell me anything."

He had fallen in love with one of the girls in his program. And because of that, we had to break up.

* * *

The train horn sounded deafening and, in that moment, erased all our good memories.

All I felt was betrayal, shock, and pain. I don't remember the train ride home. I don't remember the next week of high school.

First love is both beautiful and tragic. We feel the magic of oneness, of finding our other half. We feel safe enough to be ourselves. All that oxytocin from human touch and connection for the first time, and add on teenage hormones.

And when it ends, our worst fears are confirmed. I wasn't good enough: physically, mentally, emotionally. This other girl must've been everything I wasn't. That heartbreak triggered what I now know was a depressive episode.

If I could, I'd wrap my arms around my teenage self and say,

> *"You're okay. He doesn't know what he's missing. You are so much stronger than you think! You overcome pain and suffering, and you accomplish all your dance dreams. You meet your equal partner in love (who is way more caring and beautiful than this guy), and you become a good mom. Your pain will become your purpose. You inspire other people who are hurting as you are, and you help them to heal."*

I'd send her this message with urgency because every moment counted that week.

As an adult, I now see that this was my first deep dive into the addictive pull of codependence. I had dabbled in it through seeking validation in academics and dance, but this was the full dose of intoxication. Because he loved me, therefore, I was able to "love" myself even for a moment. But codependence is a trap: looking outside ourselves for love, peace, and happiness. The well always runs dry in the end.

That heartbreak led to the worst day of my life.

* * *

I remember hearing as a child that my uncle had taken his own life. People had said, "At least he's at peace now," and "He is no longer suffering." In this depressive episode I wasn't thinking clearly and believed that perhaps it was true. I internalized that maybe ending it all was my only choice because I could not make the pain stop.

I just couldn't shift my mental state. I cried and cried, thinking about the pain I'd cause others, but I saw no other option.

I bought a bottle of Tylenol PM from the drugstore near my house. I had just gotten my driver's license the year before. I drove through town to my best friends' houses. In my heart it was to say goodbye, but it seemed to them a lovely surprise, just coming to say hello.

It was getting dark out, and I went home. I said goodnight to my parents, told them I loved them too, and walked straight into my bedroom. I turned out the lights, sat at the edge of my bed, and looked up at all my star stickers on the ceiling: "In space no one can hear you scream" written in glow-in-the-dark puff paint. A tagline from the film Alien that I felt connected to, both for its sense of isolation and the peace that it evoked for someone who was tired of feeling pain.

Then, rather mechanically, I swallowed a lot of pills. I'm not sure how many, but at least half the bottle. I lay down in a fetal position, face turned toward the mattress.

I remember minutes feeling like hours, my heart racing, but then followed by the sensation that I was falling asleep. It was a different kind of falling asleep, though. I experienced a dissociative leaving of my body. The lightness was relieving but also frightening.

I'm not sure if it was solely fear, maybe an angel's voice, or God, but I like to believe it was the latter two.

I rolled over to look up at the ceiling, which had become fuzzy, and heard, "Get up, Nicole."

For maybe the first time, I listened to no other voice but my own intuition, and I stood up. I went out to the living room and, somehow, told my parents what I had done.

* * *

Panic ensued. My mother rushed me to the ER.

Seven minutes away. I just needed to stay awake for seven more minutes.

Burst through the doors. Charcoal pills administered. Violent detoxification. Psych evaluation after psych evaluation. "She may need to be hospitalized." Judgmental glances from a nurse who knew me from my old dance school. Psychiatrist and psychologist appointments.

Eventually I was sent home on psychiatric medications. There I waited in a limbo of shame and regret. The school was informed.

Next thing I remember, I'm with my principal and drama teacher in tears. No one realized I needed help. It was a shock to all.

My best friends are crying. My mentors are crying. My mom is crying. Now everyone was crying. Like a contagious disease, it was as if my sadness had spilled over and infected everyone I cared about.

"How could you do this, Nicole?" No one said those exact words, but the subtext was as deafening as the train horn.

How. Could. You.

Fear now. I felt like I had made a bad situation worse.

And yet, somehow, that rock bottom moment was the beginning of everything that became my life's purpose, deepest work, and what I believe to be dharma.

* * *

If you're still with me and any of this resonates with your story, I want you to take a deep breath now.

My hope is that by vulnerably sharing my truth, you can begin to release the shame you've carried about your own story too. Because the collective truth we share is this: until we admit that we need more help and support than we are currently receiving, we will continue to feel stuck, sick, and tired. True healing is not a magic pill. It starts with an honest, sobering look at what we struggle with.

At the end of the day, there are really only two directions we are travelling in life: one is in the direction of growth and healing, giving us more life force, and one is in the direction of decay and neurosis, taking us closer to illness and eventually death.

I realized after leaving the ER and slowly reintegrating into my high school life that I did not actually want to die. It was a day of intolerable sadness that caused me to make a bad decision, a true mistake that shook me to the core.

But then, I had another shot at life. Maybe my cry for help was received and I would get the help. Perhaps this time I would learn to love myself more, be grateful for the gifts around me, share my heart with only those who would hold it with care, and learn to express my emotions in a way that would be heard.

I remembered under all the stress and pressure of life, I actually wanted to live more than even wanting the pain to stop. I had temporarily forgotten. Not in a careless "lost my keys" kind of way, but in a mind-altering, literally "losing my sanity" way. The depressive episode had clouded the mirrors of my mind and made me believe that ALL was bad. Nothing was good. This sort of black-and-white thinking is so dangerous on many levels, something I remind my clients of weekly.

I re-remembered that there were such good things in my young and promising life. I had big hopes, dreams of dancing in New York City, adventures around the world that I wanted to live out. Those morsels of life kept me focused to keep going.

Admitting that I needed help and could not do it alone was pivotal. A journey of nontraditional healing through somatic and yoga therapy with compassionate role models ensued. I slowly fortified a glimmer of light in my heart that could never be fully extinguished.

No matter how "bad" things have gotten since then, even in the lowest of lows that would come and go, somewhere inside me, a voice had woken up, and it kept whispering: *Just Keep Moving.*

> *That's when I began to understand something I'd later come to teach: feelings aren't the enemy. The sensations I had tried to avoid, deny, or numb were actually messengers.*
>
> *A painful moment carries a charge of energy. Sensations build around that energy, and an emotion forms. Then come thoughts that try to make sense of it all, layering on top. We begin to make belief systems from the thoughts that feel stuck and permanent.*

Learning that sequence changed everything for me.

Beneath every unbearable thought was an emotion; under that

was a sensation. And beneath every sensation was a wave of energy moving through my body, asking just to be felt, not fixed. No wonder I couldn't think my way out of my pain because it hadn't started in my mind. I just had to keep the energy moving, tuning in to my body.

Because if I could feel what was really moving in my body (the core level energy), maybe I didn't have to keep living at the mercy of these old stories. Maybe there was another way through pain and suffering.

* * *

For so many years, I thought healing was about "figuring it all out." I believed that if I could just think my way through it, work harder, become more educated, eventually I would find contentment, happiness, and success. But my body never stopped speaking its disagreement. It was just that no one had ever taught me how to listen to "her" (my body). That's what I do now through Power Within Healing.

Whether I'm supporting someone in a somatic coaching session or holding space in a retreat circle, I help them come back to their body. The place where our history still lives, waiting to be witnessed, seen, and heard.

I've learned trauma isn't just about *what* happened to us. It's what memories are frozen in time and didn't get to resolve or move to completion. It's what stayed stuck in the body when it didn't feel safe enough to release.

> *Sometimes it's tension in the jaw from all those angry words you weren't allowed to express.*
>
> *Sometimes it's a tight belly from an expectation of perfection you could never seem to fulfill.*
>
> *Or a constant deep, wired exhaustion from surviving a chaotic family environment that keeps you playing small decades after you moved out of the house.*
>
> *That frozen glare behind your eyes that won't seem to*

thaw no matter how much someone says they love you, always looking out for the other shoe to drop.

Somatics is both the field, the practice, and the state of awareness that brought me back to myself. It's not just a modality; it's a remembering of self. We literally re-member the energetic "members" of self that have become fragmented or disowned. It is a way of surveying our internal world and slowing down enough to listen to the signals our body is sending about where there is pain or where something is still held.

In a somatic state of awareness, we begin to notice the sensations, thoughts, feelings, and emotions that are interwoven with what memories live inside, especially those we may have needed to forget to survive. These practices allow us to access more information about the ways we've been carrying our experiences.

* * *

That's why I named this work the Power Within Healing. Because the solutions to healing aren't "out there." They've always been here, living inside us—in our bones, in our breath, in the sensations that never lied, even when we had to lie to ourselves. Healing can be a simple daily charge and discharge process, like how an animal might shake its fur and run after hiding in fear from a predator and then go on about its day. But how do we do this healing safely and intelligently as human beings?

After working with thousands of women over the last decade and finding the common threads, I decided to call this somatic coaching and energetic healing practice the Embodied Purpose Process. It includes four spiraling and nonlinear stages: Ground Down, Direct Your Energy, Hear the Call, and Forward Momentum.

Ground Down

When I work with clients and students, we start by learning to return to a state of presence over and over again. A regulated place where we can think, feel, speak at the same time. We circle back to the foundational tools of pausing, breathing, finding ways to be with what is arising without overriding it.

We learn to notice a trigger and all its component parts. To pause, listen, and move the energy through appropriately. To make new choices, especially in our relationships. Learning to respond instead of react. The more we practice this, the better we feel, improving our individual well-being and that of our relationships, giving us back life energy, again and again.

While we might begin with tuning into our environment and selves to find a sense of safety, once we notice the breath and what is arising, we venture more deeply into the energy body.

Direct Your Energy

How and where are we using our energy? What is our energy like? While tracking the sensations that arise in our physical selves, we begin to attune on an energetic level to the mental and emotional selves.

The energy centers of the body aren't just an esoteric idea, though they are based on sacred ancient wisdom from Eastern traditions known as the chakras. They're also intimately connected with our nerve plexuses, those intricate highways of nerves running through the spine and branching into our organ systems. There are key points along the spine where this energy concentrates and amplifies, drawing our attention.

You may not notice subtle changes elsewhere, but you'll more likely feel strong energy towards the spine, like a change of heart as a shift in the center of your chest or anxiety about something someone just said in the pit of your stomach.

Take a moment. Sense into the center of your body. What's happening there?

A tightness, tingling, temperature change. Maybe another sensation? Is it more a feeling or perhaps even an image?

Take a breath. This is called tracking and tuning in. The basics of somatics. Let that go and practice it anytime.

Our body, attuned for survival in the "pack," constantly seeks safety, understanding, and belonging. The energy centers are like antennas doing the translating and recording of what's coming in. These energy centers become the gateways to our yes's and no's. The places where we are open flow and grow, or begin to close off, shrink, and hide.

Developmental psychology has even mapped core human needs to these centers, combining Eastern and Western wisdom to show how unmet childhood needs and trauma create energetic imbalances that persist.

These aren't abstract concepts to me. They are places I've learned to return to for deeper contemplation again and again when I feel lost:

1. *Root Center* (perineum, tailbone, running down both legs): "Do I feel safe enough to be here? In this body, in this moment?"
2. *Sacral Center* (sacrum, hips, womb): "Can I feel what I feel? Even the messy stuff? Am I allowed to have wants?"
3. *Solar Plexus Center* (top of the stomach and diaphragm): "Where have I given my power away? What boundaries do I need to hold myself with care?"
4. *Heart Center* (around the heart and lungs): "Is there room for both the grief and the beauty? Can I stay open without disappearing into the other?"
5. *Throat Center* (throat, neck, jaw, esophagus): "What part of my truth is not being expressed? Am I safe enough to listen?"

Hear the Call

The *Third Eye Center* helps us access a place of nonduality, where we can slow our minds from the polarity of good and bad and hear more accurately the truth of our intuition.

Trauma has a way of making us feel minimized, small, like we're not enough, and like we cannot trust ourselves. But it's just not true. You are enough, and you can trust yourself. You are worthy because it is your birthright, period. And there is great power in bridging that gap between where you've been and where you are now through deep listening and presence.

Contrary to some critics, reconnecting and listening to these energy centers through somatic practices hasn't turned me or anyone I work with into someone we're not, but rather who we have always been at the core!

Healing is a literal reclamation that your story also matters. A reclaiming that you have a right to feel the way you do about your past and how that may affect your fears and doubts for your future.

No one else has been you. No one else can be you. That is your greatest wisdom in life.

* * *

If something stirred in you as you read this, your body might be speaking and hoping you'll have a listen now too.

So I'll ask you what I often asked myself in those quiet moments:

1. What might shift if I stop resisting the experience and just listen?
2. Where am I outsourcing my worth right now?

And perhaps, most importantly, after some slow, deep breaths:

3. What do YOU need, Body?

You don't need to wait for everything to fall apart before you begin. You are allowed to feel, be, have, and do what you feel called to. In the healing process, there is absolutely no need to feel rushed to be "fixed" because you never were broken anyway.

You are allowed to return to yourself step by step, whether it be by a breath-filled victory one day or by a trembling, grieving loss the next. Even in the ups and downs, life is about feeling the one single present moment at a time that is the thread of your existence.

Pulling the first string in a tightly bound ball may start an unraveling. But unraveling creates movement, and movement is fluid, and fluidity is health. Stagnancy actually causes disease. So allow a sequence of growth and change to begin here and now with the awakening that you are here on this planet right now for deep meaning and purpose. Make a promise that you will not turn away from yourself from this moment forward.

There is a power within you that's always been there. It's still there, and it's ready to rise. Ground Down, Direct Your Energy, Hear the Call, and pick it up. Keep listening to the most important voice you'll ever hear—your body's.

Does it matter if you call what you hear the voice of your body? Or your ancestors, your angels, your intuition, God, or something else? What I've come to find after all these years is that it doesn't. What truly matters is if you haven't yet, I do hope you hear your own version of "Get up, Nicole," and very, very soon.

To each of us, fully living out our one true precious life while we are blessed with it.

About This Book

This is a book about remembering our God-given perfection. Told through the voices of women who have walked through fire and found their way back to themselves, this anthology offers a new map for healing. One rooted in embodiment, soul wisdom, and radical self-compassion.

These are not stories of overnight transformation, but of a slow, sacred return. To voice. To breath. To feeling. To the body's knowing.

Each chapter reveals how trauma, grief, loss, illness, or burnout became an unexpected threshold, a new beginning in their life. From near-death experiences to spiritual awakenings, from childhood wounds to reclaimed creativity, these women show what becomes possible when we stop running from our pain and begin listening to the wisdom within it.

As leaders, mothers, space-holders, visionaries, and healers, they've not only walked the path of transformation, they now guide others along it.

At the center of this collection is a shared truth: feelings aren't the enemy. They're messengers. And your body knows the way home.

This book is both a torch and a trail.

For the woman in the middle of the storm.

For the one who forgot her voice.

For the one who thought she was too much or not enough.

For the seeker, the space-holder, the one who has never quite fit in.

<u>This book is for you. And your time is now.</u>

About Nicole Smith Levay

Nicole Smith Levay—named Woman to Watch by She Heals the World—is a transformational retreat leader, executive coach, and international speaker who helps high-achieving women, leaders, and organizations move from burnout to breakthrough. Through her integrative approach that blends somatics, meditation, and breathwork, Nicole empowers people to regulate their nervous systems, reclaim their energy, and realign their work with their deeper purpose.

A former professional dancer turned somatic therapist, Nicole holds an MA in Somatic Psychology from the California Institute of Integral Studies. Her own journey from perfectionism and depletion to embodied leadership informs her work with thousands of clients worldwide. She has facilitated at premier healing centers, including Kripalu Center for Yoga & Health, Imiloa Institute, Ghost Ranch, and Mount Madonna Center, and delivered keynote experiences at women's leadership conferences, professional industry gatherings, and international wellness events.

Nicole is the founder of Power Within Healing, a community and methodology dedicated to helping high-achievers stop over-giving on autopilot and fully live their purpose. Through her signature program, Forward Momentum, she guides clients through a four-step embodied purpose process that has helped leaders, entrepreneurs, and creatives move from exhaustion to inspired, sustainable success.

She also trains the next generation of mind-body practitioners through her Breathwork & Meditation Mentorship and Body Wisdom Somatic Movement Certification. Graduates consistently share that her trainings are "transformative," "confidence-building," and "magic," noting Nicole's ability to hold safe space, personalize her teaching, and inspire them to trust their own instincts and voice.

Nicole's mission is both deeply personal and widely scalable: to create spaces—whether in the retreat room, the classroom, or the boardroom—where people can return to themselves, feel their aliveness, and lead from a place of clarity and inner strength.

Follow Nicole on Instagram and Facebook @nicolesmithlevay or connect at thepowerwithinhealing.com. To book her as a speaker or workshop facilitator, please contact her directly at nicole@thepowerwithinhealing.com or (646) 926-0304.

Adventures in a Life of Healing

Cyndy Wulfsberg

When do we need healing?

Always.

Young and in love

Home from school for the holidays, and so is he. Wondering what he's doing now and when he will call? Gran is holed up in her room. Big Bro couldn't come home this year. Dad works and works, home and away. Mom bakes into the night.

He called! And he visited this afternoon and evening. TV night. Cozy, kind of. Cold coming on.

Date night! Loved the Dance Co. and dinner at Gusti's! Just great. My idea, but he went along gladly, I think. Tomorrow AM parental command performance breakfast will be hard. Headachy from cold or one too many. I never used to drink anything but a little champagne.

Dinner at home with parents out and cocktails before Cary's New Year's Eve party. Fun except for the over-drinking and crashing hard. Not really a date. SO crowded.

He called and visited to watch bowl games and join for family dinner. I swear they like him more than me sometimes. Fat and frustrated tonight. Tense and possessive. I WILL NOT BE. Not attractive.

He called 2x with plans changed. He spent the day alone, and so I did too. He is aggravating because he always gets his way, and he forces my choices even if it hurts me. And he KNOWS I am unhappy and still does it! It just is. Too bad.

Great day with dinner and movie. I'm straightened out on my bad mood. He is wonderful.

He called 2x! Happy, happy! Gran says he reminds her of Grandad. A big, gentle guy.

Dull day. Didn't hear from him. His folks got home. No idea what went on over there. No idea what went on here either. Floundering without him. Should study. Can't focus.

Called him finally. Had been touchy about not seeing him. Time is short. He eventually came over for sundaes and games though and even planned for tomorrow! Fun night.

He called and came over for lunch, and it was fun, and he was desperate to see me! He will be crazy after three weeks! Me too! And he called later. No phone privacy anywhere.

He came for lunch, and we went out to a film series! We've been especially happy all week—wish he didn't have to go. He is weird about my interim trip. Not doing what he is comfortable with? But why? What does he want me to do? I never have a clue.

Our plans for lunch fell through because his car broke down. Reunion is over and did not end well. I already wrote him a letter and probably shouldn't mail it. I cried a little. Brutal. I miss him already.

Lonely day—I love him just bunches.

Young love is a lot about chemistry and how we ride the wave of it as it splashes all over ourselves, those we desire, and those in our way. If we are lucky, we live with people who recognize the challenge and don't pour gasoline on the fire that we are busy stoking or smother the fire and the young lovers to the point of suffocation.

When a person in love, or in hot pursuit of it, is so focused on another person that they forget to tend to themselves or lose curiosity about the effect the relationship is having on themselves and those around them, are they well? Balanced? Even OK? Who notices their condition and does anything about it to deliberately promote personal wellness?

How did the young woman care for herself? Did she know she needed care of any kind apart from wanting repeatedly larger doses of her desired one? Did she do anything to blow off steam? Did she allow herself any distraction or reach out to other people? Since I was there, I can tell you that she did not do a good job of self-care. She did not go running to enliven her body away from him. She did not call other friends because back in "the day" there was only one phone, and she didn't want to "tie it up" or miss a call. She did not leave the house for the same reason unless her parents directly asked her to go do something. She was oblivious to her family's interest in her because her visit home was not to see them but to see him. She did not think for a minute about how she felt except in reaction to him. Drowning in hormones, she had no idea if there was something she could or should do to help herself feel better and notice the effect she was having on herself and others. Her laser focus on him excluded any vision of herself. She ached, suffered, cried, and obsessed. It was a powerful addictive need, unmet and unseen for what it was.

The best thing she did for herself was to write about it. Writing became an exercise in self-awareness. When words pour out onto a page without edits or thoughts about what anyone else might think, some truth may unconsciously emerge. Or it may not be truth that emerges, but frustration, anger, and vitriol that need to be expelled for survival of the core of your character.

Do you have a way to dump out pain that is poisoning you? Can you acknowledge thoughts and feelings without editing them for correctness? You can't learn from your life without seeing what is real. Do you have a mirror for reflection? Does it show distortions or reality? Can you live your healthiest life without knowing what is shown in the mirror? You are the one who is best positioned to take steps to improve the clarity of your vision and the image the mirror holds.

Mortality

In my dream, my grandmother, newly widowed, watched her belongings float away, and as they went, she began to disconnect from her life, untethering. The small, rented home she lived in for fifty years was the warmth of her neighborhood. There were nicer houses, but hers had the honeysuckle vine enclosing the back stoop and the screened-in sleeping porch for hot nights and her daughter, who brought home litters of kittens. Her black cat, Cotton, was long gone from his perch atop the black and white TV, and the crocks of homemade beer on top of the kitchen shelves had bubbled away. I lay on the sofa bed in the living room, bathed in the cool gale of the water fan in the window, and saw it all drift off. Family and friends she would barely hear from again swooped in and took what they wanted. Her favored stepsister took some treasures she would never use and left behind a subtle sting that Gran was past noting.

I saw the things go. I didn't see Gran start to fade, but she was beginning to go too.

When Granddad died, it was a sad time for my grandmother, but he had been ill, and in my teenage eyes, it looked like he was not having any fun and could not live long. Mainly he was so alone. He had been lively and interested in everyone, and now he was silenced by his stroke. I sat at the puzzle table with him, quietly but together. They had lived in their modest house and supported themselves and raised my mother and uncle amid lifelong friends and family. While they lived their lives and were dear to us and many others, they were different from me. My grandmother never drove a car, never had a job, never wrote a check or opened a bank account, and had only flown on a plane once in her life. I had already done all of those things, and I was fifteen.

After my grandfather died, Gran occasionally visited her old haunts, but she moved in with my parents and me, thousands of miles away from where her home had been, and both my parents were working hard and were little company for her to keep.

The last time I actually spent with my grandmother, I was twenty-six and visiting her in the hospital, and she spoke to me of how nice it was there with all the butterflies flying in her room. I looked around thinking there might be mobiles or stickers on the windows, but I didn't see any. I was glad that she could see them because she had been shut up in the hospital for almost a month. She may have imagined them out of an extraordinary instinct of self-preservation, trapped as she was in an unfamiliar place, but more likely it was the oxygen deprivation she suffered due to emphysema. She started smoking in her twenties, cool and fun-loving as she was, and unaware of the price to be paid. Despite her smoking, she lived to be 76—through the flu epidemic, the Great Depression, and many wars; bore two children at home and was never hospitalized until she suffered a heart attack the last month of her life.

My grandmother's death got my attention. I started routinely counting the difference in years from her death to my age and counting on the likely time I had to live my life. I did that with anyone I knew well who was older than me. My parents and my brother were part of my mortality equation and when it was likely to affect me. My essence was alive, but apparently not eternal. The ultimate inconvenient truth delivered by Gran when she was completely out of it. I was pregnant when she died, and while that gave me comfort that life goes on, it also dawned on me that another human would soon be depending on me for theirs.

When we are faced with reality that shakes us, what can we do? Denial and the many methods of avoiding unpleasant facts are handy, and other people facing similar unpleasantness are quick to grab our hands and encourage us to be blind together despite clear immutable truth. Humans are all in this together, aware of our mortality and living with or without faith of an eternal life, with and without willingness to plan even minimally for unanticipated early exits, or sadly slogging through life doomed to suffer, anticipating more suffering, and delivering more suffering to all we meet.

Healing from this weighty awareness involved more conscientious care of my physical body even as I was losing control of it through my pregnancy. I was a dancer and was used to working to make my body able to bend to my will, stretching my limits and strengths. I had a keen sense of bodily awareness honed by hours of training and attention. Pregnancy brought the shocking loss of conscious physical control and required growth of trust in my human nature. It was amazing and traumatic at the same time. I was gradually adjusting to the physical truth and counted on delivering a healthy baby to prove to myself that I should trust my nature even if that meant I had to acknowledge that mortality was real for me too.

My body showed me the way to live, and it continues to teach me when I turn down the volume of my life and listen to it. Pregnancy temporarily forced me to listen, but it remains too easy for me to drown out the messages my mortal body repeatedly tries to tell me. Part of my adventure in healing is to practice listening to my body. Just like anything I want to do well, it takes time, effort, and a perpetual search for guidance and inspiration. I have sore muscles in my shoulders as I write this, too long working bent over. I have things to do and push through despite the late hour, the headache, or the living person in the other room who wants my attention. I close myself into stuffy spaces to accomplish tasks I deem essential when the breeze is blowing outside and the flowers smell divine. My will and my agenda often work against my ability to hear what my mortal body is saying to me every day. Can I hear it whisper, or will I wait until it screams? I have repeatedly experienced the terrible waste of denying my physical needs until my body crashes around me, forcing me to withdraw to lick my wounds. If I take care before the crash, I might not lose one of my precious days to major repair work.

Is your body talking to you? Can you hear it? Why won't you listen? What's in the way? Is it possible to take a breath and notice what is really happening and who is responsible for the physical abuse? Is it you? You have only one physical body. You are the caretaker. Are you taking care?

Sisterhood of Wellness

Imagine that you have a group of people who are available to stand by you and see you no matter what. What if those people would answer your text and forward it to everyone they know? What if they hear your frustrations and fears and share their own with a chuckle, not trying to fix yours but being in the world with you, swapping stories, and embracing you with their shared experience. They aren't always your best friends. You may not talk with them more than a few times a year, but if you call, they answer and give their time and attention to you. Sometimes they seem to know you need them before you do. Your posse. Your network. Your safety net. I call mine my sisterhood. There are men in my sisterhood too, but I think of the group as behaving like the best sisters might. I don't have any actual sisters, so this is my idealized concept, but I actually have this sisterhood in real life! I didn't know I needed it, but somehow it grew from my curiosity about others as I struggled with my own chaotic existence. I looked around and wondered how everyone was getting through it all, and I couldn't hide my need.

I was new to the community, and it was the first day of school for my first child entering kindergarten, and he had not been attending school in the US very long. He was young to be entering school, but I was aware that I needed reinforcements to match his curiosity and energy. He needed more people and challenge and order and expanded curriculum and I knew all that intellectually but worried his teachers would not understand or appreciate him. How could they?! He had lived abroad and spoken two languages and was not excited to be still or obedient.

I held it together as he got dressed and happily bundled his supplies into his backpack. We walked to school, and the crossing guard smiled, and there were more and more children heading down the street. Finally, there was the class line-up outside the building, and the kids were waving, some were crying, and parents were taking pictures, and then he was gone. I didn't cry until he was out of sight, and I was astonished and kind of horrified at the wave of emotion that engulfed me as I entrusted the human I had raised up to the grand age of five, to strangers.

I felt a touch on my shoulder. "Want to join us for coffee? You just moved in, right?" The woman had no tears in her eyes and was not struggling with composure. "Your first, right? I've been there, but this is my fifth, and I can't wait to have a few hours to myself and try the new coffee shop on Main Street. You ready?"

I drove to the coffee shop. I met four other women and started to organize where they lived and who their children were and where they were in their own adventure of family, freedom, and hopes for the future. They were a varied group, some working and some staying at home, but the first day of school is a big deal no matter what. A rite of passage I had acknowledged for my son, but not for me. It felt natural for us to bond over a big day and loosely plan to connect with one another. I needed them for sure, and possibly they would need me someday too.

Someone saw me, recognized my feelings, and reached out. Someone had done that for her once and would do it again in different circumstances out of the commonality of our human condition. When we see each other, we can help. It is easier if we are not committed to hiding our feelings. I had a "sister" who was there to help me cross a threshold that day, and people continue to help one another as we have done throughout time. We are social beings, and we need each other for healing and to be well.

I am not best friends with that person, but I started to grow my community that day, and we continue our connection despite distance and time apart. As an author, I pop up on social media with a new book and hear from people I haven't thought of for years. Who helps us walk our paths? What does it take to develop a sisterhood like mine? A sisterhood with changing membership depending on availability and shared experience. And will they really be there for me next time? Will I be there for them? Every day we have opportunities to be curious about other people, and we share the need to be seen and heard even if we are concerned about embarrassment or privacy. Do you take a moment to connect? Do you hide behind platitudes or share the truth of the moment rather than repeating the conventional scripted dialogue? If you do, you can have a sisterhood too, and it's a shared recipe for healing.

Legacy

I received a letter from myself today. It made me smile with memory, warmth, and encouragement, and brought out a little chuckle. As a writer with a file cabinet filled with a lifetime of reflection and storytelling, I am used to the experience of reading my voice from another moment in time. It always ignites memory, which I treasure since so much of our life experience sifts away like sand into the sea. Once written down, there is a record. I lived. I felt. I suffered. I loved. I healed.

I don't receive many letters from myself, but if you can arrange the logistics, it is worth the exercise. I wrote this letter while attending a retreat recently. I had tried writing to myself once before but was so self-conscious about the act that I could barely write anything! Imagine! Being too self-entangled to write to yourself! We routinely talk to ourselves and reflect on interactions with others and endless lists of daily activities, but the act of writing, putting pen to paper, can be a step too far. What was I thinking? Will someone see this? Is this true? Is it awful that I feel this way? What would my mother/husband/boyfriend/daughter/God think about me?

The first time I tried to write to myself, it was a platitude, dashed off while feeling peer pressure to complete the exercise. When I received my letter six months later, it meant nothing other than the event was recalled momentarily along with the confusion and unease that I had experienced at the time. Not a bad thing to reflect about from a place of distance and with the help of a prompt. Noted: I was there, and this happened, and I felt something. How do I feel about it now?

Time passed, and I have changed, as has my social environment. The letter I received from myself today I remembered writing with a smile. The retreat had been unstructured, and the freedom was significant for me. I wrote with enthusiastic capital letters and exclamation marks, reminding myself of things I want to do that I tend to delay. I complimented myself and used endearing personal terms that I have coined. As a lifelong seeker and fan of short-lived phenomena, like shooting stars, northern lights, lava eruptions, and eclipses, it has made my acceptance of my short time on earth as a physical being one that I consciously embrace. I called myself "A beautiful short-lived phenomenon!" That may not bring a smile of comfort to anyone but me, but the message was just for me and meant to be a reminder of my opportunity to live the life that I intend to live. I want to live so my legacy will exist past my own physical existence, offer information to those who come next, and be an intentional curation of my relationships and experiences. As a friend and mentor has taught me to consider, were you there at all if you leave no trace? Writing it down makes it so much clearer. You get to define yourself with your words.

I recently published a book and workbook after closing the estates of four family members called "*Ghost or Guardian, A Guidebook for the Pre-Dead, Do these things before you die so your heirs won't hate you later*." It is a humorous book in many ways and offers the "pre-dead" a concrete choice: clean up your mess and make some plans or deliberately torture those you leave behind and leave like a flame thrower. I even offer suggestions for post death torture of others so you cannot help but get the idea. My dearly departed had not deliberately left me in a smoldering heap, but some days I felt I was standing in a steaming one and might be sinking!

I wrote the book while grieving, working overtime on the business of others, when I was swamped already with my own messes. I was again dealing with chemistry, which bubbled threateningly with sadness, depression, and guilt. And the mortality thing was filling all my head and heart space. Too many hours in dim lit, dusty spaces, hunched over piles of everything that can be piled up eventually drew some screams of rebellion from my physical body, which actually forced me to take long, long, long walks until I finally noticed the birds in the trees and the late afternoon light. Once I recovered enough to breathe deeply, I rushed to my friends who would stand with me. My sisterhood came through big time. No one could fix it or step in and do it for me, but they could make me laugh at the end of the day and walk miles and miles with me until I could land tiredly on the living room couch and let my physical being take over and begin my repair.

After all the dirty work was done, my sisterhood again stepped in and encouraged and helped me get my book published and sold as a best seller but most significantly, they appreciated and thanked me for sharing my story. That's the legacy part. Passing it on.

Do you have a legacy you treasure and want to share? Are there favorite recipes, photographs, treasured books, objects, or stories that have meaning for you that you want to preserve for others yet to come? Possibly even others you don't know and will never meet? As a human on Earth, you have left physical traces of your existence. Is your legacy deliberate? Is there something less tangible you want to share? A belief? An understanding? An idea?

Part of my legacy is my conviction that life is an adventure of perpetual search for wellness and constant need for healing again and again. Each day, each month, each year, each trauma, loss, injury, and insult all require that we seek wholeness once again so our adventure will continue. The ease and happiness that we want to enjoy exists in our dreams and fleeting moments, but in real life we find joy because we persist in searching for it, and we keep spreading our own knowledge and experience of life so others can have more of the good and suffer less of the hardship. The fact that the adventure continues and there is never a time when life can be trapped and wrapped in paper and tied tightly with string is really the best part. Wellness and healing are not static goals but living tides that we get to seek out and ride for our lifetime. There will be troughs and crests, shadows underneath us, and challenges crashing all around. It's all part of our unique journey of seeking wellness and healing, each in our original way. The next big wave is coming, and it will be brand new and yours alone, so keep your eyes open and live your adventure.

About Cyndy Wulfsberg

Cyndy is a writer who draws on earlier work in teaching, consulting, national and international marketing, elected public office, and lobbying. She enjoys traveling to speak on recurring themes in her writing, of building a legacy, and of encouraging others to tell their stories.

Her best-selling book, *Ghost or Guardians, A Guidebook for the Pre-Dead, Do these things before you die so your heirs won't hate you later*, is a humorous look at cleaning up the mess you are making in your life before you leave it to people you claimed to love. The challenge? Choose to be a ghost or a guardian, and if you choose to be a ghost, get creative and deliberate about the suffering you leave to others. If you are aiming for guardian status, she outlines the planning needed based on her experience closing four family estates. With a background in sociology, extensive travel, and love of languages, she enjoys engaging with others wherever they are and broadening her perspectives. She is a beekeeper, animal lover, and avid reader, and lives in Michigan with her family. She can be reached through her website, fromthefilecabinet.com.

Aura

Margaret Burns

Before I was able to see what was really hurting inside people and how to help them, I had to get over my fear of seeing the spirit world, which was really the world itself. I had to get over my fear of the world itself.

I was born after a snowstorm and lived my early years in the cold weather, the kind where the wind feels brand new in each moment. Sensations followed me wherever I went, so also a deep need for hibernating, curled up as if I fit in a seashell, yet sleeping so fitfully that my teeth clenched and grinded on tectonic plates, molars sharpening wildly on their own.

And so my childhood went like that, though I did not break easily, nor could I feel the edges of where I stopped and others began because the world clung to my skin like static. And so I was always hearing things: movement, walking, whispers, music, ghosts of things trying to get my attention as the world went on swirling around me. In the beginning, I didn't mind being thrown about in the swirling because wherever I was thrown, I fell down softly like shaken snow. And soon I trained myself not to feel the cold, though it was still there when I walked into a room alone.

To better feel the air, I have always loved driving fast. When I was five, I rolled down the window of my dad's tan Ford and sat on its ledge. We were on the highway going 55 mph, and he didn't notice me for a while. I just wanted to feel free, to feel quick, windy. That day in the car, my mom held her hand out to me gently and asked me to come back, and so I did.

I was frequently mistaken for much older than I was. I was already too many years into my young age to be able to live in the world the way I was supposed to. I was just being me and not even able to hide it; really, though, I would have, had I known how.

But I was used to absorbing the world like big watercolor paper. I hid all the hard parts deep in my bones. I was at the same time both shy and unconcerned about how I appeared to anyone. It was an intensity that can only be described as a strain on my heart, both the love and the fear. The strain sometimes just knowing I was supposed to be here.

But it was not always tightness. I also loved swimming in water, fast, where I could stretch out into softness. I would go with my brother where the waves were roaring and light green. Once I got pushed (or pulled) under the water and bumped beneath rocks. My head swirled so that I didn't know which way was up, only that it was as if the sun had gone out. But I could hear a voice say, "Float." The wave washed out of the rocks, and then I came out, too. My brother held out his hand and asked, "What happened?" I was a little dizzy. "How did you get out?" he was breathing fast and almost crying.

"A ghost helped me," I said. "We can go home now." That was the beginning of hearing spirits, or at least, the first time I noticed.

There was also the ability to feel for ghosts in school bathrooms and old buildings, or in my ear next to me, to see the past in a person's eyes, to smell kitchens in other places far away, like my grandma's, before she died.

And I just wanted one thing. One thing that was part of me that would never, ever change. But energy collapsed in on itself in a big black pile, and the rest of the world seemed to move with heat and shadow. So I held it heavy. There was nothing else to do.

As a teen, I loved the book, *Are You There God, It's Me, Margaret*, praying for God to help me with MY body, and to meet a boy with clean fingernails. My timelines were always freezing, thawing, moving ahead, backwards as I tried to return to places that felt like home. "An unusual amount of déjà vu," my parents would say when I told them, "I think I'm here again."

Pushed through unseen doors and out of cocoons I had built myself, warm, bright, and fuzzy, scared of the outside. I had every right to be. Golden-tinged auras mixed in with the absolutely horrifying loudness of anything that crossed paths with my senses: color, saliva-inducing sweet taste of sugar that exploded in pink in front of my eyes, the clatter of deep darkness. Everything always magnified by color and sound and light. But also, I was brave enough to see it.

I grew up carrying this bravery with me, and then one day, I became a mother. In my labor, I saw rainbows and felt the howl from my belly echo wildly as the toroidal current of my body folded in on itself, replicating my lifetimes of birthing and becoming, birthing and becoming. The sensitivities in my eyes only got brighter after that, and stayed, and because of this, I waited for someone who could help me understand all my lifetimes.

So the shell of me came, and I felt sort of like the ones I would find on the beach. The ones that were weathered, cement-looking, cragged, white-gray, and hard, but somewhere still porous. I would pick them up from the thick, sinking sand and hold them up to the red setting sun in front of me. I held them in my hand tightly, feeling them break the skin because I was water-weary and cellophaned. The waves would push into my legs, and the wind would blow. I could have been just dust and bone, with a heart like clay and no blood left in it that broke apart in a sandy sort of way. But after becoming a mother, I was not afraid of death, not afraid of pain, just very, very mindful of the wind.

Because I needed someone to help me, you might do like I did and go see a shaman outside Marfa who will offer you some mysterious drink "for the pain." I insisted I didn't have pain till I left her yurt office and carried my baby with me back to the car, limping again from my bad hip, then remembering I could feel the hurt and wishing I had taken her advice. She squeezed my hand, and in that moment, I felt understood, about my whole life, maybe. She would tell me to stand in front of a tree until I could hear it speak to me. When I asked her what that would sound like, she said I would feel it in my heart. And then anyone who came to me with pain, I would feel it in my heart. So I became like my ancestors. To help people for whom weather only feels like air. To help them understand.

I could feel it in my heart, and then, also, I could see their insides. So I would have to stand on a hill in my backyard and look up at the dark sky between tall skinny trees. I was trying to escape from the leftover pictures and noise. Planets and black wind swirled around me and then stopped, and it was so still I thought maybe I'd died. For a moment, I was left alone, and I felt light again, like I could float. Far away constellations reached me as they went bleeding like the shapes of starfish, and air moving like some kind of tide. When I heard the spirit world speak to me, it felt like fast tattoos anchored in my chest, buzzing with pain, their broken hearts with wings. But ever since their words have been carved on my skin, I had been becoming myself.

I always felt like myself when I swam underwater on my back, just below the surface, wondering why I couldn't just live there, see the world above as wavy and out of focus and unimportant, and instead stay touching the nearby soft sand and blow air out hard through my nose, the power of loving my own breath. The water was all the way down blue, a blue as deep as a jewel. My limbs looked that color, instead of white like a ghost after a healing, giving life to what I thought was stale blood. The water hitting my skin felt salt-heavy, the waves made of mortars and pestles. When I came to the surface, I breathed in, and for a moment, I felt the air even more. Then the wind would come, and I could feel the water withering away, and I wanted the feeling again, especially around the time of the sunset. After sunset, the moon was there, too, and I could tell it was pulling the tide and changing the shore somewhere, wetting the sand and salting the earth. The tattoos, the pain, the world, the ghosts, are a part of me forever, yes. Waxing and waning, always waiting for them to show their fullness. But I was no longer afraid because the world, it was my one thing. Yes, it was always this way.

When you stand in front of me, I will hear your ancestors. They will tell me to wrap your heart tight and send light to bend into your bones where they have been broken over time. Time will stop, and you will start to remember. I will see old scars, lifetimes of them. You will remember what it is like to swim deep to the center of you and then come back and take an automatic deep breath. When you ask why life has to hurt, I will say, this is what bodies do when they change and are put back together in a new way. You will see it will all be for you. It was always for you.

About Margaret Burns

Margaret is a transformational coach and retreat leader, herbalist, kinesiologist, trained midwife, certified birth and postpartum doula, yoga teacher, Reiki Master, meditation and breathwork facilitator, craniosacral therapist, Spiritual Practitioner through Arvigo Institute with a Master's degree in Poetry and Philosophical Theology and a focus in Biomedical Ethics. She is a Female Founder with Hive Global, a certified Health Coach with the Institute of Integrative Nutrition, an upper belt in Taekwondo, and a licensed bartender. She is grateful to her parents, who have always supported her, and above all, her daughters, who taught her everything about unconditional love. She loves you, too.

The Breath Between Our Generations

Stephanie Joong

When I turn thirty, I will start showing signs of mania and lose control like my mom. This chemical imbalance in her brain is bound to be passed down to me. This is my fate, no matter what, try as I may to lead another kind of life. I should achieve as much as I can now to get ahead of those later years. If I avoid talking to a psychiatrist, then I can ward off a diagnosis like my mom's. I am the daughter who pushed my mom over the edge to mental breakdown, over and over again because I am difficult. I am a bad, bad kid. This is all my fault.

I held a few nasty beliefs about myself that I allowed to steer many of my life decisions, like the one I made to live a child-free life. Outwardly confident and accomplished on paper, it took me years to piece together what I really thought about myself deep down.

I don't think I realized how commonplace mental illness was because, growing up in the upper-middle-class suburbs, everyone kept these matters a secret. Any whiffs of dysfunctional Asian American family dynamics that resulted were buried. The immigrants did an expert job at keeping to themselves to acclimate, fit in, look the part, and do what they could to survive. Oftentimes, my parents, aunts, and uncles hid the painful memories of their past. They didn't want to burden us. Without many details, I was told my grandparents fled communist China, shedding everything they had, and began new lives in Taiwan, where my parents were born and raised. The family's journey continued to New York City. The singular focus was to improve their legacy's position in terms of wealth, education, and career advancement.

Keenly aware of my parents' sacrifices and emulating their workhorse habits, I followed the familial path to a successful career, one in which I looked like a model employee in the corporate world, able to adapt and manage change. But every now and then I questioned: *Was this all there was? Was this what I truly wanted? Was I even proud of myself?*

I'm not old yet, but I do have a mature soul, and at this point it can be quite scary to try on anything new; it takes real guts and a lot of reassurances. I sometimes wonder if I'm not entirely sincere when I say to audiences seeking my advice that I'm a lifelong learner. What I mean is this: I like learning new things when the stakes are low (pickleball, for instance). When my reputation and image are on the line, however, I'm going to revert instinctively to the old me, the old skillsets, and what I know to be comfortable, familiar. I have essentially convinced myself that I am one who gets excited about change and I'm highly adaptable. Big companies value highly adaptable employees. The global business world is so chaotic and fast-paced, we need people who can be quick to change and are even excited to pivot so we can make more money and get more business.

I started getting mixed up and seeing some conflicts in my view of myself. I found I could adapt well to changes, but when I thought about it more deeply, I realized it was only when I was the one in charge of making the change happen. When I'm the concertmaster and matters are in my hands completely, I'm powerful and make it all happen. That's why being a director has suited me well: I know what's going to happen before it even happens. And, like a good student, I'm highly trained in the techniques behind change management, so I can walk the bigger organization through a challenging transition, helping to pace everyone else. When I'm at work, I seem to barely remember what it was like to be on the other side. It turns out I like change—on my terms.

So, in this way, I've come to realize the average director will do just fine managing change because they are given the answers beforehand, show up to the meetings, and follow the script. (All the control freaks out there are now wondering if they've been giving themselves too much credit for how they adapt to change in the corporate workplace.) *What about outside of the corporate workplace, then? How well could I stand up to big changes hurled at me, beyond my control, rather than me playing the role of initiating some strategy?*

I started feeling less and less special.

I was a total hypocrite.

The one set of circumstances that always turned my world inside out and left me struggling for air was a manic episode from my mom, no matter my age. My mom was diagnosed with schizophrenia and bipolar disorder when I was a tiny child. The illness was always lurking below the surface, and then suddenly there would be these wild shifts in behavior, displacing me, throwing me off course, without warning. It was like dancing around a real Jekyll and Hyde situation.

There were, thankfully, long stretches, several years, when no episodes appeared. In those stretches, our days were steady, fewer stressors were hanging around, medication was finally dialed in, and we didn't have to talk about the bad days. Every year that I was gone for college and away from my mom was like this. Normal. And I often think of that cause and effect, how my absence brought stability and peace to my mom during those four years. I often come back to these thoughts: that I stressed her out and aggravated her condition.

When the stressors weren't manageable, there could be months of instability in our house. The manic episode and break point came in a sharp blast like a sudden storm, but took a much longer time to dissipate, leaving behind shakiness for several weeks, even whole seasons. There had been times of extended hospitalizations, outpatient treatment that shifted back to inpatient, then de-escalated back to outpatient, and so on. It was a milestone when I learned how to drive (and learned the directions to my mom's psychiatrist's office and the nearest the hospital three small towns over). The whole house would be kept awake, hearing the sounds of midnight vacuuming and the big furniture movements echoing off the hardwood floors. The cleaning and purging sprees were the clearest evidence that we were spiraling. I'd lie in bed counting the number of days there was no sleep, worry about what expensive belongings were being given away, wonder when the right time to call 911 was, because sometimes the paranoia was still below the threshold of being able to check her into a hospital against her will. I'd then get up and go to school the next day.

I dislike talking about my mom and our relationship because it is so sad when I know it used to be quite different. She expertly braided my hair in French pig tails with her shiny, manicured talons and thin, dexterous fingers. She signed me up as a toddler runway model at a children's clothing store to show me off. She came up with creative craft projects and encouraged art lessons. She had snacks ready for me when I came home from school, and the only times she wasn't home were when she was checked into a hospital. She brought me everywhere—her mini me. I was a huge part of her life.

And even when I entered my high school years, our days were closely intertwined, more so when my parents divorced, with my dad moving to the other side of the world. Then, my sister headed to college and moved out, so it was just the two of us. My mom gave me twenties to buy makeup at the mall with my friends. She drove me to tennis lessons for over ten years and wouldn't say anything about my failures when I lost matches. She dropped off take-out lunches at my high school when I turned my nose up at cafeteria dining. She quietly slid home-cooked dinners across the dining room table for me while I studied long hours for all my AP coursework. She gave me space to choose where I wanted to go to college and where I wanted to pursue a career. And when I experienced my first major romantic breakup, she found me uncontrollably crying in the shower and made herself ready to just sit with me on the couch.

On the few occasions when I tell a close friend about my house of mental illness, I end up carrying even more sadness (theirs) and pity. My helplessness momentarily returns to me, a sudden wave of needing to be taken care of. I stayed silent about my everyday home situation and treated those private matters like a big secret. The first friends I opened up to were from 7th grade; we were huddled in the downstairs bathroom of my childhood home. It's hard to believe that until the age of twelve I kept this part of me completely hidden from my persona. I cried to them, mostly in shame, because it was weird to have a different family. Fast forward ten years, and I found myself in a related situation with a college friend in my first apartment in Raleigh. She overheard me on an unexpected call from a cousin saying my mom was saying strange things, that I should check back home. Fifteen years after that, I was with two college friends in a wine tasting lounge in Healdsburg, the only customers in the place, revealing more about my past. They had known me for so long, yet my mom's health and any details from my childhood just never felt right to bring up. *"That must have been so hard for you."* But it wasn't hard at only one point in my life. There were whole seasons I existed without any real footing. I tried to convince myself that I was doing an admirable job holding everything in.

Growing up, I convinced myself that her illness was solely hereditary and that both my sister and I would end up sick one day. I was too scared to learn more about all of the factors that contributed to her diagnoses. When meeting with her case managers, doctors, and nurses, I didn't ask any questions, like, *What does this mean for my outlook?* I didn't even ask my mom. I just knew I couldn't pass these genes to another generation. I also saw what having children did to my mom, the stress that I put on her, and so, from an early age, I never had the desire to have children of my own.

When it came time to pick a path as a grown-up, I became an engineer, a practical career that would always be in demand and could make good money right out of school. I chose a highly employable path. I made fast career advancements fueled by perfectionism and a craving for achievements. I became engrossed in leadership coursework and I leapt at every opportunity for a promotion. I was highly ambitious, committed to my career, and moved to California to follow a promising job. It was through my years working in corporate environments that I solidified the belief that you earn more credibility when the words "I feel" are replaced with "I *think." Better yet, cut to the chase and just state what you want to say—come out with it already. Be direct; stick to the facts. Feelings can lead you astray in making important business decisions.*

After a long stretch of relative stability, the rising stress of my grandmother's quickly declining health, plus the isolating effects of the COVID-19 pandemic, accelerated my mom's inability to take care of herself. In this state of chaos and emotional instability, she made a series of heart-wrenching, irreversible financial decisions, edging closer and closer to homelessness, and I could no longer look the other way. I was appointed as her power of attorney.

By taking responsibility for managing her finances, I took away all her credit cards and gave her one tied to my bank account for close monitoring. I became responsible for all her health decisions, too, and put her in an assisted living home on the West Coast so I didn't have to book cross-country flights now that I was in California to check on her. I thought I was acting responsibly. I was cold. And mostly I was furious. The actions I took were robotic, completely lacking any compassion. Asian culture says I should have moved her into my own home permanently, but I wanted to stay away from her. In an act of self-preservation, and the American in me, I sought another way so I didn't have to deal directly with the consequences of her declining health. With her aside, I could carry on with my life and the growing demands of my job. My role was to hold the family together and this was the only way I could tolerate.

I never considered my upbringing to be a real challenge because I largely blocked out the most painful memories and focused on all the things (mostly material) that I possessed. For the longest time, only my relatives knew about my mom's illness, and since we didn't talk about it, none of them expressed feeling sorry for me, like I was owed anything. I took my family situation as the cards that I was dealt: there couldn't have been another way, so dreaming was pointless.

In an alarming number of ways, my privilege in this world was quite obvious, having a significantly boosted head start from an early age. Growing up, I was never bullied; my parents kept me well-dressed, well-fed, and I drifted between friend groups easily, a chameleon. Whoever you wanted me to be, I could be. I was raised in a crime-free neighborhood where the most scandalous activities might have been buying weed in my driveway from adolescent dealers and sneaking out of the house to smoke at the park late at night. On more than a few occasions, I had the town cops show up to my house to break up underaged parties that grew wildly out of hand. I made friends naturally and easily but still felt the need to stay popular, well-liked, so having the kids higher up on the social ladder over to party was my ticket. Usually, these escapades happened while my mom was heavily medicated in her bedroom upstairs or checked into a hospital overnight to force her to get sleep. Meanwhile, my dad was overseas starting his own business, an eighteen-hour flight away from stopping me from joining in on traditional teen havoc. You see, I never got into any real trouble. To think, I could have been beaten as punishment for acting out this way and I wasn't. I knew classmates with violent, less forgiving parents. I grew to think that this freedom I was afforded was my privilege.

On my way home from a summer job in Jersey City, I got into a three-car collision. The first driver slammed on the brakes to avoid hitting a loose tire in the road. My reaction time was just quick enough to also slam on my brakes, but the driver behind me must not have been paying attention. That car crashed into mine and mine got pushed into the car in front. In total shock and, thankfully, only with the tiniest hint of whiplash, I let out big, indecipherable sobs as the police interviewed me. I was dreading the amount of damage to my car. I was a mess and actually looked way worse than the vehicle. I remember the policeman calmly asked me why I was so distraught, what was I so worried about; this was clearly an accident in a highly congested part of the commute. "*My dad is going to kill me!*" I was saying this more to myself than to him. "*Your dad is going to be so glad that you're alive,*" was how he responded. And he was right. That was that. The car got fixed, good as new. I had no idea how much it cost and we moved onto the next thing. That's privilege, right?

I graduated college with zero debt, my whole education paid for by my parents. I got my first job offer as an engineer while I was finishing my senior year, and this was right in the middle of a major financial crisis when many of my fellow classmates succumbed to "fun employment." I was smart and I worked my tail off (and mostly I was lucky, attending an institution that excelled in recruiting activities with highly reputable companies). Other than that period between my May graduation and my July start date, I've never had a gap on my resume. Living at home rent-free those first years, I used my signing bonus to buy my mom a new fridge. After that, I bought myself a new Lexus. I bought my mom nice things and I made sure I bought myself nice things.

I see how my privilege from the start propelled me forward in nearly everything I took a shot at. I had a stable roof over my head and someone always having my best interests in mind available at home. This caretaker role rotated frequently from my mom to my sister, grandmothers, aunts, cousins, and close family friends. I still stayed open and curious about the world, eager to meet new people everywhere I went, studious and motivated to grow as big as I could. I had hope and knew the financial comfort I came from could help me rise over any setbacks.

I witnessed poverty in other countries as we regularly traveled to faraway places as a family for as long as I could remember. I knew enough about people coming from circumstances far more challenging than mine. I didn't have the right, I thought, to be anything but grateful. I quickly learned to suppress emotions that weren't feelings of contentment; it started early on. I had been trained to value my thinking abilities, to think my way out of bad predicaments. Feelings and emotions were to be ignored and forced back down. I saw all too clearly how my family culture and greater society treated people who appeared sad and allowed themselves to cry: criticized as too sensitive, unable to control themselves, unable to bear difficult situations: weak.

I thought I managed to rise above this stigma after a lot of self-help reading and therapy. I had my own crash and reckoning in 2018. I got pulled into a deep depression for years and pulled myself through it, even published my writing about it after enough time had passed, when I could look back and analyze where I had gone wrong. I had an identity crisis when I tethered my whole being to my job and there were workplace decisions beyond my control. I managed to untangle my self-worth from my career achievements and created a much more authentic identity beyond my day job. I started feeling good about my character and what I had to offer.

The pandemic brought mental health to the forefront. Beginning in 2020, seemingly everyone was talking about their anxiety and therapists were in high demand. Our faces looked puffy from crying and our hair was flat, molded from the shape of a pillow. I could slip into the stream and enter conversations about depression, personality disorders, and other conditions that were now okay to talk about. The doors of speaking up on these taboo topics had cracked open more widely.

After learning how to talk about my feelings, I believed I had earned some higher status of spiritual being and now I had reached a much better place with a firm foundation. There was no going backwards; that would be insane and torturous. To suffer and become enlightened only to suffer again in a slightly different way and then be brought back to peace . . . this ping-ponging was starting to feel like my own spirituality hamster wheel, which was totally unfair. For most of my twenties and thirties, I was figuring out how to airlift myself from the corporate grind hamster wheel, the professional stuff. How can there be more hamster wheels right around the corner? I was hit with genuine disbelief; this could not be the case.

How could I still feel so confused, misplaced, and searching for answers only a few years after rising from my depression? My problems had grown small with time. I became a successful adult human being. My brain held a library of knowledge that only comes with experience. I was resilient! I had overcome! I was viewed as accomplished and wise by colleagues and from my own vantage point, finally. I possessed some highly prized life skills and information: my thoughts, decision-making, and professional opinions became very valuable. People wanted to know and were genuinely inspired to know: How did I do it? What was my career journey? Any advice that I could give to someone looking for their next step at work? And it had started to sicken me a little when I responded (and why did I even think it was good for me to take these calls?) because there had been a big tradeoff for everything that I had gained. I kept a dark side that didn't reveal itself during a thirty-minute career chat. I acted like I had this flawless life and had figured out the secret recipe: Speak up about your feelings! Have a boundary with work! Cultivate your own confidence! I still carried the weight of regret and enormous shame towards my family and myself. I might have emerged out of clinical depression, but I had not yet entered the world of healing.

I practiced yoga in my twenties and started meditating with the multitude of newly released apps in my thirties. I knew when kids were throwing tantrums, parents would always remind them to take a deep breath. I still wasn't consistently managing my stress levels at work well, no matter how many miles I ran outside or indulgent vacations that I booked. My old coping mechanisms were starting to wear thin. I signed up for my first retreat in 2024 and I thought trying a 20-minute somatic breathwork session would be like getting my fortune told or a tarot card reading: something novel and fun because it was so far out there from my normal routines.

On that day I started practicing being in my body and marveling at what it could feel. I started to unwind some behaviors that had been ingrained. Before coming into the session, my body could decipher things like tightness in my hamstrings from not stretching after running and tension in my shoulder blades from hunching over a laptop most of the day. When I started the somatic breathing, the repetitive and rhythmic patterns, I began to feel much more: electricity was moving around, warmth was emanating from certain spots, a strong magnetism was humming from my belly. My breath and coughing cleared out the staleness, my hands were tingling, my thighs and ankles experienced light zaps, muscles twitching.

At the end of this first session, I was left in such a meditative state, my body was so still, I couldn't recall consciously breathing. At one point I felt like I was floating off the floor a few inches and

I didn't want to interrupt it by waking. When it was time to slowly rise up, it felt like a uniformly weighted blanket pressing down on my body head to toe, like a long slab of granite gently resting on me, securing me in place. I could release tears during this rest period, dissolving my responsibilities at work and with my family. I left that first session feeling lighter, less anxious, and appreciating myself just a little more.

I experienced such a new state of being, I couldn't believe how easy it was for me to let go of the noise and everything that I had *to do*. I sensed that I needed to continue these sessions and learn how to reconnect with my body whenever I strayed too far. I took notes and journaled after most of them to document these epiphanies that came to me when doing somatic breathing.

Growing up in a house of mental illness and the resulting confusion, pain, and chaos I experienced, I should have ended up hating the people who raised me by the time I became an adult. Through breathwork, clear and simple universal truths revealed to me that everyone is going through their own version of feeling backed up into a corner. There are times when we're all scared and feeling helpless, out of control. Images of my parents and grandparents emerged periodically during breathwork sessions, how they stayed so silent about their own hardships, and I started to gain an understanding of their experiences. My extreme resentment towards my situation and grieving the loss of any real relationship with my mom transformed into a surprisingly magnetic force drawing me back to my parents and their family and my ancestors who came before.

In my culture, it was frowned upon to be sensitive and I was rewarded for acting grounded, neutral, and compartmentalizing my emotions. Through my breathwork experiences, it immediately became clear how important sensing is and allowing emotions to come through is a necessary life skill. I used to be angry at my sister for not being able to handle family dynamics, needing to step away for her mental health, and leaving me to save the day as the younger sister. *What about my mental health, though? What about the damage that I have inflicted upon myself by not asking for help when I was underwater?* Now I can feel and use the right words to communicate with her about these uncomfortable topics. I want to be able to do this with her, to reach that point where, even though the conversations are messy, we could be there for each other. It is so much better than pretending everything is fine. Ignoring has been hard. Burying has been hard.

Through breathwork, it came to me that helping my mom is not another source of stress for me. I'm not here to rescue anyone and it's not out of family obligation. I *get* to be a part of her life and I *get* to receive her love again. Before somatic breathwork, I struggled to piece together a place to even start. I failed to see that coming back to my mom was what I needed. I didn't know what it was like to be a mother. I wondered if my mom just wanted to be my mom again. I could stop blocking myself from this homecoming that I had been missing. I had to unlearn some of my thinking habits to reinvent my story by taking cues from what I sensed from within my body, not my mind.

I first signed up for somatic breathwork coaching to deal with stress from work and to show up differently as a leader to my employees. What I actually desired was to learn a new way to deal with all of this burden. From breathwork, I ultimately changed the way I process feelings for myself and with everyone around me.

Recently, after long, deep breathing, I had a vision of my paternal grandmother, Nai Nai, who passed over twenty years ago and whose funeral in Taiwan I did not attend. I was in college and my dad convinced us that we didn't need to be burdened with her ceremony and not to make the long trip from the States because we had our own lives; we had our own responsibilities. Nai Nai came to me on the week that I was planning to visit my dad, her second youngest son, at his home seven hours away to celebrate his 70th birthday. I had planned a road trip from Oakland to celebrate his seventy years of toiling through life.

Nai Nai was not speaking. Or moving. She looked like a still, black and white photo of the way I remember her: short, luxuriously silky white hair and big, dark, round eyes. She's not smiling and she's not *not* smiling. Peaceful, she always appeared that way. She had such smooth skin. I don't remember it wrinkling; she still had the fat in the right places as I was seeing her. Nai Nai is watching me through this open channel that we've created. What's emerging is that I can love myself. She is saying that I can take what I've learned from opening myself up to the troubles that surrounded my mom. I have endured a lifetime of the pain inflicted upon me from her illnesses. I am somehow connected to my mom's pain, mine, and now with this newfound clarity, I also need to recognize my dad's.

More pain? Two parents to deal with? Two lineages of different traumas to pass straight into me and this current generation of adults? I am not uncomfortable; I am sizzling inside. The magnitude of what I feel in this channel with my Nai Nai is but a fraction of what she endured. That day opened a channel straight to this feeling I've been avoiding since the passing of all of my grandparents. I wish I knew them better. I wish I had asked them real questions. "*Your grandparents had very tough lives*" was the only bit of surface-level information given to me when I asked mom and dad. I noticed my shame, once again, for missing all of my grandparents' funerals, their last moments of breath—I'll point out that is the most minor grievance of them all—and for not knowing how to act around my parents, just hoping, silently, that they would be okay when their parents died and they would not need anything more from me. That day my Nai Nai is encouraging me to bring her love to him; I can help him with his own aging journey. Any wrongdoings of the past simply have no place between us.

What is held or stored in my body so that when I'm consciously deep breathing, I can feel movement and tension shifting? It always comes out in big tears. Most often when I'm breathing somatically, I'm giving myself a moment to create a bubble around me and shield me from my own overactive thoughts and self-created noise. It's the absence of thinking—hovering above wakefulness and drifting towards sleep, most of us can't envision places in between those two states. It's dreamlike and there's seeing, but not with my eyes. Removing the vision even for twenty minutes gives rest for the overstimulated parts of my body and brain. *So much processing and how much of that processing is actually useful for bettering myself?* What a concept, resting the overactive mind during daytime hours! Nearly every time I breathe in a session, I release tears, especially when I'm in a meditative state and allowing what needs to happen to do just that. I started crying more freely outside of these windows, too. How many years of pent-up tears are still inside my body, aging or fermenting? The release comes in the doses that I can handle at any given time. I contemplate what a full release feels like, not because I am in distress, but because I am moved to let go of something.

I can release guilt for how I behaved towards my family. I can release all the shame, acknowledge the enduring pain without minimizing my struggle for what it was, and move on to a more easeful existence despite historical chaos. I used to feel like I could never pay back all of the financial comforts that were owed to my family. It was my payment for carrying out these duties. I felt beholden to them. Filial piety often comes to mind, as there were such high obligations to my parents and filial piety served as a core cultural model for the way I was raised—to have a strong sense of duty towards one's family, regardless that the magnitude of the situation far exceeded a single soul's capacity to carry the burden. My self-worth is not tied to what I did or did not do for other members of my family.

I don't need this burden any longer; I can even be a guide for my family to start releasing their burdens and I can trust that I am going to be more than fine, because I have unearthed my hidden power. I have allowed myself reinvention and growth.

I never imagined I'd be able to have a conversation with my sister about how I was angry that she didn't do more when I was struggling, how it felt like I had no one I could count on. My husband and his parents stood by, offering to help, and I constantly waved them off; I thought it had to be something that my kin alone dealt with. Every day I grappled with this immense pressure to continue getting raises at work, in a place where I felt I didn't belong, so I could one day pay for everyone's cost of living, including both my mom's and my sister's. Every day I worked harder and took on more demands by stretching myself in every direction. It was never enough.

I never imagined I could convey out loud my deepest underlying fears. My sister feared becoming homeless like our mom and my fear was that I would have to be the one to prevent that from happening *or else.*

I never imagined I could go through a day without my family's baggage dangling over me, a constant reminder of my accumulated guilt, guilt for not being able to come to everyone's rescue.

I never imagined I could look back on my childhood and experience gratitude for now being able to feel so deeply. My sister was more than an empath. She discovered her sensing powers early on, experienced life in her body, and should have been celebrated for her gifts.

I never imagined I'd be able to open a gateway to ask for help from a source of energetic power beyond my comprehension and allow myself to receive this healing.

There is another way, aside from pretending like everything's "fine" and to keep our heads down to deal with the card we've been dealt. Finally daring to shine a spotlight on the pain that has been lingering for far too long without an avenue to escape is not an act of bathing in self-pity nor is it an attention-grabbing scheme. There is strength in acknowledging the grave reality of the situation, including all its ugly parts, and wholeheartedly owning my reactions and feelings.

I'm a prime example that overtaxing my mind for solutions to address emotional trouble held in the body just doesn't work. Feeling my way through inherited pain and listening to what my body has to say is a mechanism I had to learn to develop when nothing else was effective. Living in my head all the time, trying to solve problems with my intellect alone, made my outlook more complicated and added unnecessary stress. A simpler life is not a diminished life.

> *There is absolutely another way.*
>
> *Enormous generational pain has been passed down to me; an abundance of special talents has also been passed down to me. I can see the many choices and take agency over my decisions. I can go down a path that deviates from everything I inherited and have been*

told. My fate is in constant motion; I have endless possibilities for how to lead my life. It is far from too late for me. I don't need to run away from the fear of illness because I have this incredible power of healing.

I am the daughter who chose to reopen the pathways to love despite an upbringing fraught with instability and disruption. For the next 30 years, the next 50 years, and on to the end of my days, I have the gift of tapping into my intuition through my body and trusting the answers that come through. I discovered this intrinsic well of energy; it goes everywhere I choose to go. How special is that? I can call upon these universal messages whenever I open my arms and open my heart.

That's my real privilege.

About Stephanie Joong

Stephanie Joong is a dynamic speaker, author, and business leader dedicated to helping individuals embrace their power, silence self-doubt, and step into their most confident selves. With over 15 years in the life sciences industry, she takes pride in serving as an operational leader by day and a voice for women always.

Amplifying underrepresented stories and challenging societal stereotypes on what makes the most competent leader is a passion close to home. As a co-author of the bestselling book, *Brave Women at Work: Lessons in Confidence*, Stephanie shares her story about overcoming professional setbacks, navigating uncertainty, and emerging stronger, wiser, and with greater resilience.

As a solopreneur, she founded the Real Women Within Reach community and provides situational coaching for a range of women seeking advice to grow and exchange support. After reinventing herself more than once, Stephanie carefully measures her days with an "ALIVENESS Scale, 1–5" to counter conventional markers of success.

Stephanie's educational highlights include an MBA from the Kellogg School of Management, M. Eng. in Biochemical Engineering from Lehigh University, and a B.S. in Chemical Engineering from Bucknell University.

To learn more about Stephanie, book her as a speaker, or collaborate with her on a project in women's leadership and wellbeing, please visit her website at www.sjwithinreach.com.

You can also visit Stephanie at:

LinkedIn: Stephanie Joong
Instagram: @stephaniejoongwu

Sing your HeART Out: The Ultimate Self-Care

Samantha Long

When I was about eight years old, I discovered the ultimate self-care. I would wait until no one was home, move the furniture out of the way in the living room, and passionately perform all of my favorite songs. I would use a stool to reach the record player, which sat perfectly inside its own drawer in the Formica entertainment center that my dad had designed and built by hand. Early on, it was albums by Taylor Dayne, Whitney Houston, and Michael Jackson. Then, I moved onto my mom's cassettes—Tina Turner, Gloria Estefan, and Linda Ronstadt. These passionate performances kept going for years. All I knew was that it felt amazing.

What I wouldn't give to go back in time for just one day and experience music and movement through the body of that 8-year-old girl. The subtle vibration of each note moving its way from my gut towards my throat and outward felt like an internal massage of my organs. As a Somatic Self Care Coach, I have studied the nervous system and parts of our physiology at length, and I now know that singing offers, among other benefits, the practice of diaphragmatic breath. This type of breathing allows the diaphragm to move downward completely with the inhale so the lungs can more efficiently fill with air and also lets the air exiting from the lungs travel through the voice box (trachea and larynx), creating a stimulation of the vagus nerve and activating our parasympathetic nervous system, allowing for a state of presence, calm, and connection. This is the same state we can access while in deep meditation, as well as during yoga practice, zen moments of art making, and other types of passive or active rest. No wonder it felt like I had cracked the code to life!

The lyrics and messages of these songs brought on their own unique sensations. Empty aching for an oddly familiar heartbreak. Fizzy, excited curiosity about a romantic love I hadn't yet experienced. Feeling both the empathy and connection, I co-regulated with these "strangers" from a far distance through music. I scanned the little lyric books tidily enclosed within each CD case and sat in awe at the artistry. On my own in a house that was often filled with loud arguments and angry silences, I was far from alone. Whoever wrote those songs, I was right there with them in it. It didn't matter if I understood the exact experience; their expression was felt and received on my end. Engaging in music or other arts can synchronize our physical and emotional states, creating a sense of connection and safety. Many yoga instructors and wellness practitioners like me will incorporate music into sessions because it can be particularly helpful for individuals who struggle with self-regulation or emotional expression.

By age 11, my taste had evolved with the times, and the Goddess herself, Alanis Morrissette, had descended on this Earth. She was not only a vocal innovation with a sound I had never heard before but also my introduction to the emotional expression of the rage against the patriarchy. Suddenly, it didn't feel quite as hard to be a young girl in the 90s.

Singing felt like I was really onto something, which I now can translate into those first few glimmers of authentic expression that just feel so right, like the body taking a giant sigh. In these moments of pure, uninhibited self-expression, I experienced myself authentically. Filled with confidence and passion, without self-judgement, I went for the big notes and found, to my pleasant surprise, that I sounded great. Yet still, I waited until no one was around to enjoy my newfound pleasure and hone my craft because even at that young age, I had learned somewhere along the way that you had to be good if you were going to share your art.

For years, I only performed solo shows to an empty living room, privately practicing this personal self-care only in moments when it was safe, until one day I was ready to be witnessed. I told my mom that I wanted to be a singer. I proclaimed it without much apprehension about the response because it just felt so right that it couldn't possibly be wrong. *Wrong.*

"You'll never make any money doing that unless you're the next Celine Dion!" my mother blurted. The "gut punch" was felt through my whole center. An emptiness formed in my belly as the naturally creative piece of my being was snatched out of me. I froze as the messages settled in. "Not good enough." "Not acceptable." "Be practical." Of course. How silly of me. My bid for recognition was met with dismissal. My attempt at self-expression was met with suppression. My move toward expansion was met with resistance. So I shrank. My mother had never heard me sing and she wouldn't until much later.

* * *

Physician, author, and speaker, Dr. Gabor Maté, defines trauma as "not what happens to you, but what happens inside you as a result of what happens to you." Trauma is not the challenging event itself but the internal wound or disconnection from the Self that results. Trauma interrupts self-expression. When something is too fast, too much, or too soon, our stress response is activated. We can fight (stand up for ourselves or argue) or flight (run away). Sometimes we freeze (avoid or procrastinate), and often we fawn (appease or blend into the background). Illustrated in Maslow's *Hierarchy of Needs*, recognition and self-esteem are so important for all humans as a means of survival and self-fulfillment. In a world where "being successful" is defined by a series of boxes to check off, we will shrink or morph in any way needed to fit in. Even if it means letting go of entire pieces of our identities. Our natural bodies, our sexuality, our uniqueness—all on the chopping block in order to be accepted, liked, or better loved.

If needing to sing as well as Celine Dion was the minimum requirement to be recognized as a bona fide singer or to even "waste" my time trying, I would quit before even moving ahead.

And I did just that. My mother's discouraging words were not a malicious attempt to steal my joy and squash my magic, but her own trauma rooted in fear. This is this same collective past trauma that lives on inside me, which I have the burden to heal from and privilege to learn from every single day.

That day may have shut down "Singing Sanctuary" temporarily, but it didn't affect "Music Island." If you did not quite get this reference, here is your enthusiastic invitation to check out Pixar's *Inside Out*. The movie personifies and normalizes the beautiful spectrum of emotions we all experience as humans and illustrates how our entire personalities are formed by our experiences. My personality was undoubtedly affected that day. I learned that unless you're going to be the best, then don't even bother. I learned that I should fear judgement because not everyone will accept me. I learned that you can't just do something because it feels good and that if you're going to put energy into something, you have to be able to "make a living" doing it. These limiting beliefs took hold inside me over the years as I absorbed more and more examples of how life was "supposed" to be lived. I learned to choose how I spent my time "responsibly."

Thankfully, at the same time that I was exploring singing and marveling at the talent of lyricists like Noel Gallagher and Sarah McLachlan, I also began writing. I loved to write in my diary, however sporadically, penning odes to my friendships and crushes. I wrote short stories and poetry and very often song lyrics. Writing was easier, as I could keep it confined in the safety of my notebooks but also because I could receive positive feedback about this particular pastime. It was deemed a more responsible use of my energy, an activity that could "more realistically" lead to a career in journalism. I remember the joyful faces of my father and grandfather when a short story based on the life of my grandmother was chosen to be included in an annual calendar for a local senior living community. "You can become a newspaper reporter one day!" (Heaven forbid, a book author!) The words felt safer, and so they stuck.

I went to college, got a degree in communications with a concentration in broadcast journalism. Upon graduating college, I learned that an entry-level production assistant role in the broadcast media industry would pay approximately $20k annually, which even in 2006 was not enough for me to commute and feed myself, let alone pay rent. How responsible of me to have strived towards this career endeavor instead of becoming one of those "struggling artists!" (Insert eye-roll for sarcastic emphasis.)

Ultimately, I landed my first job in the sales department at a major book publisher, and my career blossomed. Around that same time, I met my now-husband and moved into a tiny studio apartment in Union City, NJ. At $750 per month, it was all I could afford. It came with an exposed brick wall, a cool fire escape for smoking cigs, and a few baby roaches, and it was all mine. With a roof over my head and a budding, new relationship, a newfound sensation of groundedness set in. With the space all mine, I found myself again in that empty house. I sang in the shower, while I cooked, while I cleaned. I sang while watching live performances of my favorite artists on YouTube. I invited my friends over for drinks and apartment karaoke. And I felt a curiosity stirring once again. How can singing be somehow less responsible when it's so clear how much humans love music? Had I known then the words of Amie McNee, author of *We Need Your Art*, I would not have had to ask that question. As Aime so beautifully teaches us, "Wanting to be a successful creative is not childlike or foolish. It's valid, responsible, and doable. Taking your art seriously is not irresponsible or silly. It is what you are here to do. It is needed. It is responsible. It is generous. It is good."

* * *

Singing and making music had sat on a dark, back shelf for 15 years, but something was starting to re-emerge. It started innocently with bar karaoke, which evolved to more intentional karaoke in my apartment. But I started singing again. My college friend, fellow music lover, and biggest supporter, Matt, encouraged me and even provided loving yet constructive feedback. As a casual music producer, Matt learned how to find instrumental tracks and how to use editing software. Sitting inside my sister's acoustically amazing walk-in closet, we started recording covers of 90s songs and popular dance hits like "Stereo Love," and Lady Gaga, of course. It was pure magic for our friendship, but it was more than that—it was my chance to learn to trust myself again.

We dubbed ourselves 5AM (taken from a line in Pink's "Raise Your Glass" with a similar look to the acronym for Sam And Matt). We were even able to secure a few live musical performances, including the Jersey City Pride Festival in 2003. What a cool opportunity! Yet at the time, I had my reservations. Without a live band accompanying us, we would be performing to a backing track, a recording of synthesized instruments, including recorded background vocals. Though this approach is much more common today, at the time I wasn't sure how it would be perceived. I was terrified that people would think I couldn't sing, an echo of old fears I had internalized. *Would the audience think I was lip-syncing? We don't deserve to be here. Who do you think you are – the next Celine Dion?*

I went from excited to extremely nervous. I couldn't eat the day of the event, and as I stood in the "green room" tent on that 90-degree day in August waiting to go on, my body started to say no. Nausea and severe cottonmouth set in. With the security net of my two closest friends by my side, I chugged a bunch of water, got on the stage, danced, and sang. We had a great time, and so did the crowd. For the rest of the day, people stopped me to tell me how great the performance was. No one asked about the backing track. No one questioned my capabilities. I had moved in the direction of something that seemed unsafe, and I not only survived, I thrived. Basking in the reality of moments like that is how it's proven inside our bodies that, as author Glennon Doyle puts it, "We can do hard things."

I continued this dance with discomfort for years. It was awkward to meet up with other aspiring musicians to discuss collaborating. Singing in front of strangers was anxiety-inducing. Singing in front of friends or family was even more nerve-racking. In a world where we're taught that our art has to be approved or stamped "good enough" in order to be worthy of showing off, it can be terrifying to open yourself up. I constantly questioned my dedication to this art in particular and would often hear my inner bully question, "Who do you think you are?" Not good enough. But the reason I kept going was my friends. Find the people who will actually see, hear, and witness you. Surround yourself with those who will not judge but meet you right where you're at. Those who will not warn you to turn back or shrink down but empower you to grow where there is room to expand.

People pleasing or fawning as a trauma response is a pattern many of us learn early on, instilled by a fear of not being liked or accepted. When we've had past experiences where expressing our needs and showing our authentic Self has led to negative consequences, we will seek to manage how others perceive us by shaping our behavior and actions to please others. We want to be good enough for everyone else, and in the process, we often not only forfeit our own internal experience and sacrifice our own needs but also our own creativity.

In regard to performing, I spent years doing just that—morphing my voice to emulate popular vocalists in order to be received well. I would hold my vocal abilities to standards that were often unrealistic and judge myself harshly when I couldn't hit those high notes. Looking back, there were definitely many "cringe-worthy" moments. The ones that still pop into your mind randomly even five or ten years later and cause a visceral tensing of the body and even a grimace to appear on the face. But there were even more moments where I felt the fear, moved forward anyway, and proved to my brain and body that I could in fact trust my natural intuitive nudges. If music and singing felt so good to me, even through the fear, they were to remain in my world always.

* * *

Trying yoga had been on my to-do list for a while. Since my early 20s, I was already experiencing muscle tension and exhaustion from hours at a computer and lots of work travel. One summer evening, I took my first yoga class after work in the Flatiron district of NYC. I was surprised at how easily I dropped into the moment and followed the instructor's cues. My tension began to melt, both physical and emotional. Between the guided movement and intentional breathing, a clearing occurred, and by the end of class I had discovered a new form of self-care that worked for me.

Yoga became a staple in my world for the next few years. Up until then, I had not found a physical exercise that I enjoyed. I hated the feeling of my heart pounding inside my chest, whether I was jogging or sprinting from my door to the corner to catch the bus to work. I was never an athlete and never had much enjoyment from pushing my body through physical discomfort. The reduced pain and enhanced mental clarity I experienced with a consistent weekly yoga practice were undeniable. Something was starting to click.

Years later, yoga saved my life during one of my hardest transitions—being laid off while eight months pregnant with my first child. The sudden loss of my career really rocked my mental health. While moving through lots of grief, anger, and fear, many long pauses, deep breaths, and introspection kept me aware of my safety and connected me to the present. Now having a better understanding of physiology, I have no doubt that the extra constriction in my body that comes with anxiety played a role in labor difficulties and the inability to have a natural birth. After my beautiful daughter arrived, love filled the house. My husband and I experienced typical new parent anxieties, which called for more presence, more connection. I turned to my yoga practice following birth and slowly started my journey back to embodiment. It wasn't long before I decided I would one day become a yoga teacher and share this powerful healing modality with others.

* * *

Ancient scriptures define the practice of yoga as the journey of the Self, through the Self, to the Self. The practice is meant to support us in reconnecting to ourselves by way of presence, regulation, and embodiment. My current favorite explanation refers to yoga as the OG ("original gangster") of nervous system regulation. Yoga asks us to slow down and just be. By way of promoting a feeling of safety in the body, yoga, breathwork, and meditation practices, among other forms of self-care, support the functioning of our internal systems, including our nervous system. The role of the nervous system (NS) is signaling to the rest of our biology whether we are safe from danger or under threat, essentially whether it is okay to relax or if action is required. Whether we are being chased by an actual bear or are up against a major deadline at work, the NS communicates with the other systems of the body to act accordingly for the sole purpose of keeping us safe. Your NS can also respond to a sense of danger and emotions of fear rooted in a past experience, firing off warning signs in the body, even if you are safe in that present moment.

After completing my yoga teacher training, I spent years geeking out on books and courses about physiology, trauma, and the nervous system. *Everything* started to become more clear. For example, I now understood that the cottonmouth and nausea I experienced when singing publicly wasn't my body attacking me or working against me—it was actually just reduced saliva production due to a slowed digestive system. If you're being chased by a bear or vulnerably opening yourself to potential judgment, the body goes into "fight or flight" and shifts its focus from slow, healthy digestion to increased heart rate, blood flow, and muscle engagement (or what I like to call "GTFO" mode). Intense anxiety accompanied by these bodily sensations would make me, and most people, want to run from our fears by avoiding these anxiety-inducing situations altogether. In those moments when things got really hard and scary, my body was only trying to support me through what was a perceived threat. But when we care for ourselves and prioritize healing, we can release attachment to that perception and come back into the now.

Somatic practices, such as yoga, dance, art, breathwork, and chanting, all engage both the mind and body and help to activate the "rest and digest" response in the NS, counteracting the "fight-or-flight" response. Intentionally incorporating these types of self-care into your life will also support the brain's ability to form new neural connections, essentially allowing the mind to detach from old limiting belief systems and allowing the body to release patterns of past trauma. Nervous system regulation builds your resiliency and supports you to move forward when past trauma interferes with your authentic self-expression and inhibits your capacity for joy.

Singing my heart out was never about money or fame. It was always about joy and pleasure. The undeniable sense of connection that is felt when listening to music, absorbing lyrics, and immersing in the sound elicits its own corresponding sensations. Have you ever listened to a song or watched a performance that brought on warm fuzzy feelings in your belly or a sense of opening through your heart or even brought you to tears? That is our invitation to allow intrigue and fascination to take over and to trust that your body is giving a "thumbs up." Once we embrace this and even move towards it, for example, by engaging more with the arts or even starting to let your own creativity blossom, warning signs may start to fire off. Old stories like "You'll never be as good as Celine Dion" will creep in and make your body recoil with hesitation. Obsolete programming such as "Get a *real* job" will cause you to freeze up and question your own authentic desires. In these pivotal moments where anxiety and fear are perceived but not actually relevant, a regulated nervous system and sense of somatic awareness will allow you to create space for a genuine response versus reactivity rooted in the past.

When you can move towards what feels good and right without people-pleasing or fear of judgment, there is an integration occurring just outside of the mind's eye. Like opening an ordinary door to find it's actually a treasure chest. One day when I began composing music to accompany the lyrics I had been writing my whole life, I had a moment that felt like sparkles and tingly excitement blanketing my entire body. I was sitting in front of the 88-key Yamaha keyboard for the first time since I had purchased it the year before. I stared at that beautiful instrument for a year, but I just wasn't ready. On a very rare day, when I was alone in an empty house, I sat down and reminded myself how to play the few basic chords a friend had taught me years before. Then I found that I could play some Lady Gaga songs with those chords. Eventually, I broke out my lyrics book, sang back the melody a few times, and then chose the chords that seemed to fit. A song was born! Those first moments of pure creation felt like magic, and I really liked what I had just produced. Then, the second thoughts followed: "This is no good compared to what's out there." "Too poppy." "Not very deep." I heard the words of my wounded inner child. I sat with the discomfort of those old wounds, and then I kept going because there wasn't actually ever anything in my way.

I continued quietly working on original music (which no one has ever heard), creatively building my business, Aligned Heart LLC, and slowly introducing art as a therapeutic regulation tool to my children and my clients. I also joined the Arts Council of my town at the suggestion (really demand) of a friend and local councilman. Initially I felt not like a contributing creative, but more like an asset to the group. I attended meetings and events, created promotional flyers, boots-on-the-ground type stuff. Eventually, as I settled into the group and felt more connected to my purpose, I started to let my creativity shine through. I spearheaded and coordinated an annual mental health open event and an annual town talent show—programming that offered the community space for authentic self-expression. One year, I decided to participate in the talent show I was also hosting. My brain and body persisted, "Who do you think you are?" I sang "Rise Up" by Andre Day and received some really beautiful feedback. In particular I caught the ear of a local dad, who also happened to be a drummer. He reached out and asked, "Can we put something together?" meaning, "Let's start a band!" With relative ease, we found a few other local musicians, and I asked a very talented friend to share vocals with me. We started a 90s cover band called Sam & The Fridays. We're now about three years in and play at local venues a few times a month. It brings me such pleasure to sing my favorite songs to some of my favorite people. It's something that at one point I never thought was possible. And unlike the phantom sense of fear anxiously asking, "What will they think?", the sensation of joy inside me is very real.

If you're thinking, "I could never sing on stage in front of strangers," I have good news for you. You absolutely can, but you don't have to because that's MY thing! The real question is—what's YOURS? As a Somatic Self Care Coach, I work with women all the time who tell me, "I don't even know who I am or what I want or what my 'thing' is." Understandably so, as our emotions and intuition have been bogged down and suppressed for so long. We've been conditioned to prioritize fitting in as a means to establish a false sense of security, when the way to feel truly safe is to be seen and heard and recognized in the fullest expression of our True Self.

Embodied living by way of nervous system regulation is the new witchcraft. Having a regulated nervous system is the differential factor between living on autopilot as a slave to our trauma and triggers or empowered living in connection with our Body's intuitive wisdom. It's the difference between bitterness and resentment or grounded communication of needs and desires. Between living a life in accordance with someone else's ideals or actually feeling the sensations that attract us to our true passion and purpose. Between thriving or just surviving. We know today that staying grounded and taking care of our bodies and minds are what make all the difference.

Writer and performance artist, Alok Vaid-Menon, captures the pain of suppression: "There is no loneliness like having people only see you after you've erased yourself." Maybe you've felt the nudge to explore something you put down long ago but haven't been physically or spiritually ready to reapproach. Maybe you feel an internal longing and emptiness for something more. Or were you often told you were "too sensitive" or "too much" in childhood and long to regain the ability to express yourself freely? These are just a few of the circumstances I help women through every day. Together, we walk the path from "Keeping Up with the Jones" to living authentically as yourself, from navigating a minefield of trauma responses to practicing self-regulation as a path to empowerment. It's safe to take up space—sing, dance, love, and live boldly—not for fame or gain, but because being real feels better and it's also healthier!

If you're wondering where to begin and who has the formula, the answer is YOU! Only you can care for yourself according to your own true needs. But it helps to have support in the process of reconnecting to what those needs actually are and re-establishing the self-trust necessary to stay the course. We are not meant to go through this world in silos, and further, we can't always rely on our friends and romantic partners to have the answers. You are not alone. Support, self-care, and somatic wisdom are how we reclaim our voice—and our life.

If you're feeling a readiness to explore, a stirring curiosity, or better yet some excited butterflies in your belly, please connect with me. As a somatic self-care coach and yoga instructor, I am also a creative guide devoted to helping women reconnect with their true essence. Through my classes, *Aligned Heart Method Yoga*, group and one-on-one somatic coaching, and intuitive guidance, I support women by teaching nervous system regulation, embodied self-expression, and the art of living in alignment with one's gifts and values. If you'd like to get to know me better, I encourage you to explore my podcast, *Self Care Is My Job*, and visit my website at www.alignedheart.net.

About Samantha Long

Samantha Long is a certified yoga instructor (RYT 500), Somatic Self Care Coach, and the founder of Aligned Heart Yoga & Self Care. Samantha specializes in trauma-informed yoga, nervous system regulation, and somatic movement and breathwork. Her classes focus on tuning into the wisdom of the Body as a path to remember who we really are at our most grounded and most regulated state. As a teacher and coach, Samantha supports overwhelmed and unfulfilled women to reconnect to their true essence and reestablish self-trust in order to live a more empowered, authentic, and creative life.

Stories About Web Weaving

Victoria Klum

"Spider has everything within her body to weave her beautiful web. In other words, she creates her own entire little world by accessing her internal resources."

—Kathy Harmon-Luber
(in an interview with *MindBodyGreen.com*)

I've made it a point this year to spend a lot more time outside, whether it's my morning walks along the greenways near my apartment or just enjoying a slow weekend morning on the patio. Reconnecting with nature has given me a greater appreciation for the incredible wildlife in North Carolina (how can you not believe in magic after having a firefly come right up to you and perform his light show?). What I didn't expect were the lessons it taught me about myself, along with the opportunities it has provided to heal old wounds and traumas, and to celebrate my resilience.

One recent Saturday morning, I studied a spider who had painstakingly re-woven her web on my patio (she's been here awhile and is pretty much my roommate now). I walked over to her web and watched as she put the finishing touches on her latest creation—her previous web was destroyed in one of our recent summer storms. I thought about the number of times she's had to either repair or rebuild her home, whether it was from storm damage or the bumbling human (that would be me) who inadvertently wrecks her web while tending to nearby plants. She's even traveled to the other side of the patio—a long walk on tiny spider legs—to try her luck in a different neighborhood.

"Don't worry," I assured her as she protectively paced around her web, "I'm watching out for your home this time." The spider settled back in the center of her web, and I returned to my seat. As I sipped my coffee, I felt a great deal of empathy for this little spider.

I've had to re-weave my web dozens of times. As I thought about that, I began to realize just how much of an imprint those experiences have left on me.

Only once in my entire adult life have I attempted to put my aesthetic stamp on a place that I've lived. It was my last apartment in Alameda, California, and I had lived there for more than 12 years before I brought home some sample paint cans to test out. The property manager had been encouraging me to "go bananas" with the paint colors for at least two years, excited to see what I'd come up with and assuring me that I wouldn't get dinged on my deposit since I had already lived there for so long. Even then, it was only my bedroom and the kitchen that got makeovers, although I loathed the "rental beige" walls throughout the rest of the apartment.

My aversion to decorating my apartment was less-than-charitably observed by my friend and one-time roommate: "This place doesn't look like you at all! It's decorated—if you can call it that—like you expect to flee on short notice."

Ouch! But she wasn't wrong. Pretty much everything I own is small or light enough for me to move by myself, and my shelves are arranged so that I can shove books and tchotchkes into boxes without much fuss. I mentally resist hanging artwork, even though I own (and have created) several paintings and fine art photos. I had been in my current apartment for nearly four years before I finally gave myself permission to hang light-blocking curtains. And, well, we won't talk about the number of produce delivery boxes I've hoarded that are stuffed in my storage closet (they're the perfect size for books and tchotchkes).

And as I typed out that last line, I realized I am at a full-circle moment. And it explains a lot about why I've had such a visceral distrust of the idea of "home" for as long as I can remember.

I learned early on not to get too attached to a place, but as a deeply introverted child, I desperately needed an escape from the daily hell that was part of always being the new kid in school. Even when I was sharing a bedroom with my mom, I'd carve out a corner and lovingly curate my space with magazines cut-outs and posters I got from the drug store, having saved up my allowance money to collect them. It was never fancy—obviously, painting over the rental beige walls was out of the question—but it was mine. Or so I'd let myself believe.

Usually, by the time I had my space set up, Mom would come home and tell me we were going to the grocery store, and my stomach would knot up. Mom would pull the car around to the back of the store, where the loading docks and garbage bins were. The trip signaled yet another move as we loaded as many discarded produce boxes into the trunk and back seat as we could to avoid the expense of buying moving boxes. The smell of rotting fruit would linger in the car for weeks, and I learned the hard way to not pack clothes in old melon boxes. To this day, I can barely tolerate the smell of cantaloupe.

The trip home would also frequentlly come with another lecture about using thumbtacks to hang my posters on the wall.

"We'll have to spackle all of those," Mom would grumble, looking disapprovingly at the constellation of pinholes in the wall.

In case you're wondering, no, we weren't a military family. And no, we weren't in the circus, either. It was just me and my single mother, who did her best to keep us housed, and often that meant moving closer to wherever she was working. Between grade school, middle school, and high school, I attended 13 different schools—and lost count of the number of houses and apartments we moved into along the way.

Shortly after I graduated high school, Mom was finally able to buy a house. Although I wanted to believe that I'd finally experience stability, I could never shake the feeling that this web would also be suddenly destroyed.

As much as I liked that house—and the fact that I could paint my room any color and hang all the posters I wanted—when I look back on my time there, I can't recall ever calling it *my* house. It was always "Mom's house." It just never felt like any part of it belonged to me or that I truly belonged there.

That unsettled feeling, plus being in my early 20s and ready to strike out on my own, pushed me to find a space to spin my own web. My friend had returned from a semester overseas, and we decided to rent a place (a first for both of us). It was an "old Portland" style house, and it had plenty of personality (and possibly a ghost). I worked at a real estate office with the man who managed the property, and we were friendly enough that he was pretty relaxed about letting us make *some* alterations.

Plus, it was walking distance to one of our favorite music venues and a quick drive to several others: the perfect location for two 20-something music-loving girls. It was the first time that I felt like I was home. It was also the first time I remember feeling truly secure.

It came at a cost, though: my mom was angry with me for moving out and cut off communication for several weeks. Though I couldn't see it then, I understand now the hurt and fear behind her outburst: it was the first time in her entire life that she lived alone. I don't think she really knew how to be alone, and the idea of it must have terrified her. But I needed to build a life of my own, and so did she.

We eventually reconciled, and I'd visit her a few times a week. I was still enjoying my first experience of being a grown-up and learning how to deal with issues like balancing work, school, and fun and how to keep a house party from getting out of hand (or more like, how to mitigate the damage in the aftermath).

After about 18 months, the relationship with my housemate became strained for all of the silly reasons that young people argue. That tension, plus my mom falling on difficult financial times, forced me to make the painful decision to move back to her house.

I repurposed part of Mom's basement as my living quarters so my comings and goings would be less disruptive and so that I had a little space that I could pretend was my own. I transferred from community college to Portland State and began taking evening classes. I made it a point to see as much live music as I could in an effort to hold onto the life I had started building for myself on Ash St., but the atmosphere at home grew heavier, and my nights out became less frequent.

Following her layoff the previous fall, and the months-long dispute that followed, things between my mom and her now former employer got progressively worse. Even though she had been applying for other jobs (and I was contributing as much of my paycheck as I could toward household expenses), I could almost hear the foundation cracking. So, it wasn't a complete surprise when, on the morning of my 26th birthday, my mom informed me that the bank was foreclosing on the house.

Fifteen days later, I came home from work to discover several notes on the kitchen table that led me to the garage, where I found my mother's lifeless body, along with the gun my grandfather had given her "for protection" when I was a baby.

During my life with Mom, no one really knew where one of us ended and the other began. Although her life ended on the first Friday in April 1991, it would be more than a year before I could begin to build a life that was truly my own. There was probate, selling Mom's house (her death halted the foreclosure process), possible litigation with her former employer, fighting with bill collectors, and filling a half dozen giant dumpsters with decades of accumulated crap. Her life had ended, and though I had some help from my relatives, it was mostly up to me to bring closure to Mom's life before my life could begin.

The long nights of sorting through Mom's belongings to determine what could be sold or consigned versus what went into the garbage left me angry and distraught. The things that I desperately wished I could throw out—soul-destroying grief and incandescent rage—couldn't be tossed into a dumpster. It didn't matter if I tried to gently discard them or hurl them into the bin with a window-rattling scream, they kept finding their way out of the dumpster and back into my body.

Most nights, I was too upset and exhausted to sleep, so drinking a bottle or two of wine while staring at MTV until I drifted off became my new evening routine.

In what was either a moment of clarity or a long-overdue crash-out, I got extremely frustrated one night when I couldn't rewind live television (TiVo wouldn't be invented for another eight years) and was about to hurl a half-empty wine bottle at the TV, but something stopped me before I let go of the bottle. I recognized the force: it was the same one that stopped me when I found the gun under Mom's body and wondered for a microsecond if I was meant to go with her.

"This isn't you," I heard a voice say. "This isn't your story."

It was true. "Lost, sad, angry, and drunk" was absolutely *not* the story that I wanted to write about myself. I took the wine bottle back to the kitchen, stumbled off to bed, and then stared at the ceiling until I fell asleep about 15 minutes before my morning alarm went off. As I left for work, my exhaustion was marrow-deep; I had a hangover (again) and a lot of questions for myself.

I didn't know what my life was going to look like in the coming months and years, but at least I knew what it *wouldn't* be like. That was a start.

One thing I did know was that I had to get out of that house. I rented a dingy apartment in a neighborhood that was equal parts historically lovely and quite dangerous, depending on which street you were on. I had no intention of staying there long term, but it was in an area that was close enough to my favorite music venues that I started visiting my old haunts and reconnecting with friends. I slowly started to reimagine and re-create my sense of place in the world, even if my sense of home was still shattered.

The next seismic jolt came one evening over dinner with work friends. Patrice[1], an intern who worked in my department, announced that she was taking a job at one of the Bay Area universities in the fall and was moving to San Francisco.

I had visited San Francisco twice before: my mom and I spent a night in the Bay Area on our way to Disneyland, and then again on a trip with friends a year after Mom's death.

I remember getting out of the car and having a deep sense of knowing that I would live in San Francisco one day. Patrice sug-

1 (*All names have been changed to preserve privacy.*)

gested I move there with her, and we could be roommates. I knew in my gut that I had to say yes.

Resilience rarely shows up wearing the same outfit twice. As a child, it sometimes showed up as me building my own internal worlds. In grade school, resilience was becoming a fast enough runner (mostly to avoid getting the crap kicked out of me for being the new kid in school) that local track teams invited me for try-outs. Or it arrived in the form of music or books I could get lost in until I found myself again.

As the time drew near to moving to the Bay Area and needing to find a place to live, resilience showed up in a form I had never experienced before.

Looking back, I suspect that Patrice did not expect me to accept her invitation and immediately regretted inviting me to be roommates. Even though she would talk about how excited she was for us to find a place, something felt off. Eventually, she admitted that she wanted to move into a place with her new girlfriend and basically wished me luck in my future endeavors. At that point, we were less than a month away from moving day.

Faced with the prospect of finding a place for me and my two elderly Boston Terriers to live in a notoriously challenging rental market, the easiest path would have been for me to un-quit my job (they didn't want me to leave in the first place) and un-cancel my apartment.

Over coffee, I told my friend Tom my tale of woe about my (now former) roommate-to-be. He took a slow sip from his drink and said, "I think you're going to back out of moving to California, and you'll blame it on having dogs because it's too hard to rent a place with dogs." The combination of his tone and the irritatingly smug look on his face activated the "F-YOU! JUST WATCH ME!" part of my brain.

After a loud three-minute monologue peppered with f-bombs, "how dare you's," "you don't know me at all, asshole's," and "y'all just keep underestimating me's," we finished our coffees and headed back to work. In those three minutes, I had unloaded decades of pain and anger around instability, abandonment, and being constantly underestimated by people who never really saw me at all. I had also just unearthed a level of grit and determination that I didn't even know existed.

I knew San Francisco was a main character in my story, so there was no way I was giving up on it. Not like this.

On my way home, I stopped by Safeway and picked up the previous week's Sunday *San Francisco Chronicle*. While the dogs ate their supper, I combed through the classified ads to see what was on offer. I spotted an ad for a place called Roommate Resource and gave them a call the following morning. The very friendly person there looked through the database and faxed a list of about 15 people who had available space.

Over lunch, I called and arranged a flight to SFO, booked a hotel room, and reserved a rental car for the upcoming weekend. Looking at my itinerary, I realized I had approximately 30 hours in San Francisco to find a place, and I needed to make the most of my time.

Finding a place to live in San Francisco was quite an education. I quickly got over my romantic notions of living in the Haight-Ashbury after spending over 20 minutes trying to find a place to park. I stood in a windowless closet in one flat and was told by the master tenant that I was actually standing in the bedroom. Sketchy neighborhoods, musty apartments, and $600+ for one room (my entire apartment in Portland was just over $500): things weren't looking good.

Then the Universe smiled on me. The second-to-last place on my list was a flat in the Mission District. I found parking less than a block away—a miracle—and the main tenant was only the second person I met on this tour who was awake and coherent before 3 p.m. and didn't reek of weed.

The bedroom was large and bright, and there would be space throughout the flat to incorporate my furniture. She didn't flinch when I mentioned I didn't have a full-time job lined up but had a contact at a temp agency and was sure they would keep me busy.

The only concern she had was that the landlord, an uptight Buddhist who lived in the upstairs flat, might object to my dogs. "I wouldn't worry about it, though," she said. "If he makes a huge deal out of it, you and the dogs will just stay here as my guests for as long as you need to find a better place!" We sealed the deal with a hug, and I canceled my next appointment.

I found a place to live in San Francisco with five hours to spare!

I ended up taking over the lease when Katie moved back to Sacramento to be closer to her family and I stayed in the flat for a little over six years.

Although, living in the Bay Area, I finally created the stability that I so desperately longed for, I can see now that there were times when I've mislabeled stagnation as stability. And I still catch myself clinging to places longer than I should, as if staying in beige rooms would prevent me from having my web ripped apart again.

As I was finishing this essay, I needed to stand up and stretch. I walked across the patio to check on my spider companion's web, only to find that it was gone. An upward glance told me that she had decided to relocate to higher ground. She seemed unbothered. She knows that no matter what happens, she can weave a new web, crafting each circle to suit her needs without worrying that she may soon have to re-weave her home. Everything she needs to make her home is within her.

I never knew that such a wee thing could help me witness my own resilience and show me that it's okay to embrace non-permanence while allowing myself to truly live in a space.

So, it may be time to take those empty produce boxes to the recycling center and pick up a few picture hanging kits. I may even go bananas and paint a wall or two.

About Victoria Klum

Victoria Klum spent her early childhood in Phoenix, Arizona. That would prove to be prophetic, as she has burned her life to the ground and risen from the ashes many times. A highly sensitive, introverted child, Victoria used writing and photography from a young age as a means of exploring, observing, and communicating.

A life-long sports fan, she has contributed words and photos to soccer publications including *Prost Amerika* and *Courage Country*. She currently publishes two blogs: a journal of writing and photography called *Just One More Thing . . .* (found at Vicster.net), and *Not Sticking to Sports*, observations on sports, culture, and society.

Now starting a new chapter in her life, Victoria is dusting off her arsenal of cameras, paints, and canvases while exploring life as a visual artist and returning to long-form writing that pushes her creative boundaries and nourishes her soul.

After a lifetime on the West Coast, Victoria now resides in North Carolina with her two cats. She volunteers with a local pet rescue group, writing cat bios, and starts her day with a 3-1/2-mile walk and a stop at the nearby pond for some Turtle Therapy.

Dancing Through Diagnosis

Mary Jane Thompson O'Hare

I was born April 4th, 1964, at 4:00 a.m. I have four older brothers! Four is definitely my lucky number! The reason I was born at 4:00 a.m. was because my mother and father (B.J. and Ernie) went to a movie and dinner. B.J.'s obstetrician told her they could go to dinner and a movie, not a movie and dinner. Since B.J. and Ernie ate later in the evening, the obstetrician had to wait to do the scheduled Caesarean section. The birth went well. A 7-pound, 4-ounce baby girl! After four boys!

At the time it was not in vogue to breastfeed. I was given formula. Most babies were fed formula. I went home and seemed healthy. Things were going well! Four boys at home running around, but B.J. and Ernie loved having children and always wanted a big family. Plus they were great parents! I seemed to not be keeping my formula down. I was not gaining any weight. B.J. brought me to the pediatrician, very concerned. The pediatrician said, "We will keep an eye on her." I was throwing up everything. After bringing me back and forth to the pediatrician, B.J., Ernie, and the pediatrician decided to send me to Columbia Presbyterian Hospital in New York City under the care of Dr. Singer, who stated, "We will cure her or diagnose her."

My older brothers were ages 11 to 5 years old. Every day, B.J. and Ernie would get the boys off to school. Ernie would go to work, and B.J. would take the train and then the subway into NYC to New York Presbyterian Hospital to see me. Dr. Singer was a fantastic pediatrician. I was extremely sick. Not gaining any weight. The hospital tried different smoothies and formulas, bananas, rice, wheat, beer, and all sorts of concoctions. Dr. Singer gave me hormones too, and I needed blood transfusions. Our friends and relatives volunteered to donate blood to help save me. Lots of people we knew would commute into the city if they shared the same blood type as me.

All of my relatives, grandparents, brothers, parents, friends of grandparents, and friends in the neighborhood were praying for me to get better. They prayed at church and throughout the community.

B.J. and her mother, Mary, were heavily involved in the community. They were on the board of the YMCA. B.J. was on the board for The Junior League of Monmouth County and about to become president. Mary Smith, my grandmother, was president of Family and Children's Service in West Long Branch, New Jersey. These women established how important it was to serve your community and volunteer. They preached to their children and grandchildren how blessed we all were and to give back to those who may be less fortunate. So all around the community people were praying for me.

When people in the community saw me in years to come, they would say, "We prayed for you!" I felt very blessed! They would look at me as though I was a ghost. The ladies were usually my grandmother's friends or my mother's friends. These gestures from the community and the strength of prayer made me become very spiritual and realize prayers really work, and miracles do happen!

I was in Columbia Presbyterian Hospital for approximately four months. I was not diagnosed but seemed to be gaining weight. The prayers seemed to work!

Growing up, I was a picky eater. For lunch, B.J. would pack ham and cheese roll-ups, no bread. I hated bread, spaghetti, sauce, fish, almost everything. I did love meat and potatoes though! When fish was served for dinner, I would get a fried egg.

I continued on with my life. I went to ballet on Monday; Tuesday was ceramics, and Wednesday was Brownies and later Girl Scouts. I took swimming lessons at the YMCA. I was busy every day. I actually loved having an activity after school each day. The reason was B.J. was working.

B.J. owned a children's clothing store. Ernie worked for XS Smith, which was B.J.'s father's greenhouse manufacturing business. The Thompsons were always involved in sports, arts, dancing, and volunteer work. On Sundays, we would try to get everyone to church. Wednesday night youth group at the United Methodist Church in Red Bank. We all had to go in order to get confirmed. Sunday night was a family dinner with grandparents. Sundays, we would drive down to Lakewood to visit our great-grandparents on the farm. The boys may've brought home turtles and snakes.

Ballroom dancing was for all the Thompsons from 6th to 8th grade, usually on a Thursday night. White gloves and all! Ballroom dancing was not only learning the cha cha and jitterbug, but it was learning manners and proper etiquette. Our mother loved Emily Post! She had a copy of her book, of course. Mother would state at the dinner table, "Mable, Mable, strong and able, get your elbows off the table!"

Our family loved ice skating on McCarter Pond, which was down the street from our house in Fair Haven. Ernie loved to speed skate. He had skates with those long blades. We would watch him skate around in a circle in second position (ballet style). Most of the boys loved sports, but if you did not, you were involved in art classes or volunteering, Cub Scouts, Boy Scouts, Girl Scouts, and Cadets.

We were fishing and learning to hunt too. Our mother and father loved the outdoors. Our father trapped muskrat to sell the fur in order to date our mother back in the 1940s. Swimming lessons in the summer at the beach and in the winter at the YMCA. Tennis and golf lessons when we could fit them in. Fall was football and cheering. Winter was gymnastics, swimming at the YMCA in Red Bank, basketball, and performing in the Nutcracker at Count Basie Theater in Red Bank. Winter vacation was driving to Vermont to ski. The entire family went with two other families. It was below zero, usually, but to this day, all the Thompsons love to ski. Softball and baseball in the spring with "kick the can" and "capture the flag" in the neighborhood. Springtime, we went fishing in

McCarter Pond. They had a fishing derby once a year. We also went crabbing in the river.

But also, not to forget . . . The Thompsons had a trampoline in the backyard. Children were always over. B.J. and Ernie had all neighborhood kids get a permission slip signed by their parents before they were allowed to jump on the trampoline. Summers were gymnastics camps at the YMCA. We would take a bus to Marlboro to go to camp. In the winter, this same location had ski lessons. Summer was swimming lessons and surfing! We lived about two miles from the ocean, which we all loved. The family also went to Silver Bay on Lake George for a week or two every summer with another family. We swam at 7 a.m. for the morning dip. We went waterskiing and saw a live musical on Wednesday evening.

Ernie and B.J. loved sports and the outdoors; B.J. loved tennis, Ernie loved golf and all sports. And he loved to hunt and fish. The family would eat everything and anything they killed. Including squirrel stew, which B.J. told us was beef stew. I would enter the town's fishing derby with my brother, Scott. I was told to dig for the worms the night before. Put them in some dirt in a coffee can.

I would volunteer for Family and Children's Services, helping with the luncheon by selling chances and tidying up mints. On Sundays, I would volunteer at Riverview Hospital in Red Bank, New Jersey. I had 500 hours served there. I was a candy striper and then a River Teen. I learned that from a young age we are blessed to have shelter and food on our table. I learned how important it was to be involved and volunteer in your community.

At age 13, in 7th and 8th grade, I was tested by the Royal Academy of Ballet. They would come over to New Jersey from London. The test was difficult. I had to decide if I would dance at least three to four times a week or not do ballet at all. I decided to try field hockey instead. I played field hockey in high school and later played ice hockey. I joined the boys' golf team in high school, and my coach was a great dancer. I did ballroom dancing after school and joined the dance choir for the high school musical. I loved dancing the jitterbug. I learned many different flips to the jitterbug. One over one shoulder, one through the legs, one over the back, one to the side of the hips. So much fun!! I joined the ski club and helped keep stats for baseball. In the winter, I did cheerleading for the boys' basketball team.

One day after school my teacher said, "Mary Jane, your classmates want to learn to dance the jitterbug. We will teach them how to dance after school." The teacher was Mr. George Griffin, an amazing Advanced Placement Biology teacher, great golf coach, and great dance instructor. He was kind and funny. So, off we all went. Probably six students. Three or four girls and three or four boys. Mr. Griffin was demonstrating to the class with me. All went well because Mr. Griffin was leading.

I was assigned a classmate boy to teach. Mr. Griffin demonstrated, and my partner put me up on his hip to flip me, but I was hanging upside down in the middle of the flip. Mr. Griffin said, "What is wrong?" I said, "He is standing on my ponytail!" He was standing on my hair! It was painful but way too funny! Everyone was crying, they were laughing so hard! I yelled, "I cannot move!" as I was upside down! Everyone just laughed! No one was hurt! It was all just great fun!

B.J. was adopted, so her heritage was uncertain at the time, but later on the family realized she was from Northern Europe—some English and German and other nationalities. I had mixed heritage, but my ancestors were mainly from Scotland and England. In these countries, they mainly ate meat and potatoes, so it made sense this is what my body was telling me to eat.

I was always pretty skinny. Probably because I was still sick—not really absorbing any protein or nutrients. As a child, I was a very picky eater. Mom would pack lunches for everyone, but I only wanted ham and cheese roll-ups. For dinner I wanted meat and potatoes. I hated fish, spaghetti, almost everything. When B.J. or Ernie made dinner, I was allowed to have a fried egg if nothing else seemed to taste good to me.

People thought I was just a picky eater.

Later in life, I went to college. Late at night, when my friends and I were studying, we would make air popcorn. We all loved it. The air popper would melt the butter on the top in a little silver tray. Then you poured the hot melted butter on the freshly air-popped corn in the bowl. Yummy!

One night we decided to order pizza at about midnight. I had a slice of pizza. Everyone then went to bed. I could not sleep. My stomach was killing me! I listened to my body. I assumed it was the grease from the pizza. "Not doing that again," I said to myself!

During college, I majored in business administration with a concentration in management. I took electives in art, dance, yoga, sports medicine—stuff I loved! My first yoga class was 42 years ago! It was mainly chanting and meditation, no asanas. It was to help with stress before exams.

I graduated early, hoping to do a Semester at Sea my junior year in college. I was taking five to six classes a semester to be able to go. Unfortunately, my father, Ernie, wanted me to transfer to Rutgers for in-state tuition. It was half the price! I thought by the time I transferred, and the credits didn't all count, it would be cheaper to just graduate early. I decided to graduate a semester early. No Semester at Sea, but a jump on the job market!

I worked in New York City (NYC) at The Condé Nast Publishing Company and at Ernst & Young (EY) in the theory end of accounting in the research department for the national office.

I did two internships: one my sophomore year at Ernst & Young and one my junior year at Condé Nast. After graduation I worked at Condé Nast. I started as a "rover" during an internship, then was placed at Vogue in the merchandising department. I wished I wrote *The Devil Wears Prada*—it was just like that! Then I worked in compensation for the personnel department. Realizing it wasn't paying me very well, I went back to accounting, working at Ernst & Young. I took accounting classes at night after work at Pace University.

I met my husband in New York City. We dated for three years, got married, and moved to New Hampshire for two years so he could get his MBA at Dartmouth. Then we lived in Jersey City, New Jersey, and then Glen Ridge, New Jersey. Approximately nine years later, we moved to Montclair, New Jersey, for ten years. I worked at Ann Taylor in NYC and in Short Hills, New Jersey, before having children. I worked there for approximately six years. I loved retail, fashion, and helping women look good. It reminded me of helping others at my mother's children's clothing store while growing up. I was the top salesperson in the metro area for three years—making the company over a million dollars every year for three years straight.

Our first baby was due on October 31st, 1994. We signed up for Lamaze classes, and I did prenatal exercise classes at the hospital. I went to a women's college, and my female philosophy teacher told us to have a birthing plan. "Meet with your doctor and go over a plan of what you want." The professor said it was nice to have warm water on you. "Think about giving birth in a bathtub. Try not to stay in bed but move around." Squatting was helpful because of the gravity working with you and not against you. I wanted to deliver my baby at home. My mother said, "What if something goes wrong?" Always move around; try to have a baby in a bathtub or squatting. I practiced the Lamaze birthing video every night. The birthing techniques were from the 1970s. I thought they were helpful, but the ratio seemed off to me. I decided to listen to my body and do my own ratio of inhaling and exhaling. This seemed better. My intuition helped me through all three births, but the breathing techniques helped. I had all my children naturally. No epidural.

In 2008, when the banks went belly up, my husband decided to stop working in the banking industry and go back to school. The state of New Jersey was offering a free program called "Brokers to Teachers" at Montclair State University. It was difficult to get into the program, but my husband got in.

We ended up moving to Rumson, New Jersey, so my husband could teach 8th grade math in Fair Haven, New Jersey, the school I had attended 30 years ago. Our children were going into 3rd, 9th, and 10th grade. No house yet. Family members were helping us out. I was working again at my brother's funeral home. I had been a stay-at-home mom for 15 years before this. I was president of the PTA and did lots of volunteer work. Helped with the writer's room. Ran golf outings and raised lots of money for the public school system in Montclair.

The stress of the move brought out stomach issues and health issues for me. I was in and out of doctor's offices. I had GERD. Was put on Nexium, the little purple pill. It seemed to work for two weeks, and then it didn't. I had lower back pain which, from yoga training, I realized could come from stress.

My son would rub my stomach every night—he knew I was in such pain. I had sciatica. My intuition told me to do asanas from yoga training. This seemed to help. I was listening to my body and intuition. I watched a documentary on a doctor from NYU regarding the correlation between stress and lower back issues. The somatic work seemed to be helping me at the time.

I found dance classes in Shrewsbury, New Jersey, at the Presbyterian Church. I joined the church and the dance class. I loved it. Moving and dancing felt great!

I told my brother I would work doing visitations and funerals, but I didn't like sitting at the desk all day. I was gaining weight. Still not feeling great. My doctor was trying to diagnose me. I was told to get blood work done, which I did. I was told to get an ultrasound of my organs near the stomach—kidneys, liver, etc.—looking mainly for ulcers or tumors. All tests came back negative. Good news, but I was still not feeling well.

Finally, the gastroenterologist said, "We are going to give you an upper endoscope." This is when I was finally diagnosed with celiac disease—something I had since birth!

My entire life I was suffering. What a relief to know I could treat it by diet! It was such a big weight off my shoulders. Within ten days, I felt better. No wheat, barley, oats, flour. I could have potatoes though! Also rice, vegetables, nuts, meat, fish, and poultry. Most things in the outer aisle of the grocery store—where doctors usually say to shop.

After talking to my mother-in-law and doing research, I realized I was a "Failure to Thrive" baby because I was allergic to the formula. No one knew back in 1964, but they know now. Thank the Lord! I count all my blessings! I believe in prayer and gratitude and faith! I feel very blessed! All the people praying for me as a baby—it worked. I believe in community coming together to help each other out. I believe in listening to your body, especially when it tells you that you've been sitting or standing too long!

In 2013, I got certified to teach yoga. A 200-hour certificate from Brahma Yoga in Sea Bright, New Jersey, which got washed away with Superstorm Sandy.

I was first introduced to somatic dance and Kundalini yoga while living in Montclair, New Jersey. I loved this form of expression. The instructor would put dance music on after warm-up and tell us to close our eyes and dance around—"Do not leave your yoga mat but just breathe into the moment and express yourself." It was wonderful! One of the first classes I went to was with a friend. After class, my friend said, "That was so weird! I'm never going back!" I thought the total opposite! When can we do it again?! I also did other forms of dance and Pilates with a former Rockette.

My husband and I did ballroom dancing together in NYC when we were dating and also in Montclair. We both loved swing music and the jitterbug. We felt like old souls. We loved dancing to Big Band music like B.J. and Ernie!

I feel like it was a miracle I survived back in 1964. Through prayer, community, love, and doctors—I lived!! I believe in faith and prayer and miracles! I believe that somatic dance, breath work, yoga, prayer, meditation, movement, doctors, and eating well have helped me through much pain during celiac episodes, sciatica, and other pain in my body.

I feel that the eight limbs of yoga can help you through life's pain. Whether it be breath work, asanas, meditating, or other foundations of yoga—such as somatic dance, Kundalini breathwork, or other forms of dance or Pilates. Whatever your body is telling you to do, YOU should listen!

I have continued my journey. I have 200 hours in yoga training. I am certified in restorative yoga (50 hours), Kundalini breathwork (100 hours), Reiki One, and I am working towards somatic training.

I practice each morning by praying, grounding down, breath work, chanting, and meditation.

I try to dance or play a sport each day.

I hope my journey will help you with your journey!

A few poems that capture the feelings of being alive.

Dear Lord:

I thank you for clean water
I thank you for clean air
I thank you for all the Love there is to share.

I feel so blessed to be on this beautiful earth
With all its bounty and dirt.

This Beautiful Earth
The Mountains, the trees
The bountiful leaves.

The valleys and the steeples
The variety of people

The kindness of caring
The tenderness of sharing

Let us be thoughtful and caring
And loving and sharing.

About Mary Jane O'Hare

Mary Jane O'Hare is a lifelong community leader and business professional who also shares the world of wellness, yoga, and somatic healing. After years of chronic health struggles, including a lifetime of undiagnosed celiac disease, Mary Jane discovered the power of intuitive movement, breathwork, and embodied spiritual practices. She has completed foundational training in yoga, restorative yoga, kundalini breathwork, and reiki and continues to explore somatic practices as part of her own healing journey.

With a degree in business administration and a career spanning roles at Ernst & Young, Condé Nast, and Ann Taylor, where she was recognized as a top-performing saleswoman, Mary Jane brings a grounded, service-driven approach to everything she does. She has held leadership roles in community organizations, including treasurer of Family and Children's Service and president of the PTA at Northeast Elementary School.

Today, Mary Jane integrates her love of movement, prayer, and service as she transitions into this next chapter of life, one rooted in gratitude, healing, and supporting others on their path to wholeness. Her family is everything to her, and she thanks God every day for her husband and children.

Something Ancient Unfinished Within Us

Amanda Millay Normand

There are moments in life when you feel abandoned by friends, by family, and even by those you believed would always be there. The ache of feeling left behind by others can cut deep, but then there are other times, quieter, harder to name, when the abandonment comes from within. When you stop showing up for yourself. When your own needs, voice, and boundaries are pushed aside.

This is self-abandonment, and sometimes it hurts even more than being left by someone else. It's not as loud, but it lingers deeper because losing your connection to others is hard, but losing your connection to yourself can feel like forgetting how to come home.

I have come to learn my journey of healing comes from all of these layers. People often say healing isn't linear, and I've found that to be true. Healing twists, it doubles back, it pauses. Sometimes, you don't even know you need to heal, not until your body begins giving you signs.

Trauma doesn't always announce itself either. It can be invisible. It can look like success, like business, like being the one who "has it all together." It hides in the ordinary, behind smiles and schedules, behind caretaking and perfectionism. It doesn't always come from a single, catastrophic moment. Sometimes it's born from years of subtle injuries, words never spoken, and life events never closed.

Silent and slow, it can wear a smile in public and fall apart in private. Trauma often hides in the ordinary. It doesn't have one shape. It doesn't have one cause. It can come from one event or a lifetime of micro-injuries. What matters is not how it looks to others, but how it feels to the person living with it. Healing from trauma also doesn't look one way.

My body began speaking to me the year the world started stepping back outside. As others emerged from their homes, eager to reconnect and resume life, my world was turning inward. That year, I developed a polyp on my left vocal cord. It required surgery and five long weeks of complete silence. No talking, no whispering, just stillness. It felt symbolic, like my body was asking me to listen in a way I never had before. Listening to myself was new.

The following year, in the same month, another message came: shoulder surgery. Again, I slowed down but only for a moment. I told myself to push through, to stay ahead of the pain, keep moving. I know my body well. I could fast forward my recovery by working the same fascial lines that connect the shoulder to the rest of the body.

Then came the next wave. My hand started going numb. Headaches hit with a new kind of intensity. My heart began acting up. Still, I pushed harder. I convinced myself that strength meant powering through, not pausing.

By the next spring and summer, the whispers had become screams. I lost feeling on the entire left side of my body. I couldn't balance on my left leg. My hands were numb every morning. My husband would wake with me, massaging life back into them as the sun rose. In December 2024, I finally had spine surgery. It took my body breaking down for me to finally stop and listen. To begin to truly heal. I had pushed myself too hard for too long.

After a lifetime of disconnecting from my own sensations and feelings, my body had finally reached its limit. And the irony wasn't lost on me. I'm a movement teacher. I help others feel at home in their bodies. I teach breath, awareness, efficiency, and recovery. I guide athletes back from injury, stronger than before. I talk about listening to your body like it's sacred, but I hadn't been listening to mine.

Every injury I had was from my shoulders to the base of my

skull. The very areas I rely on to teach, to support others, to use my voice, and to hold people, physically and emotionally. I teach spine health, yet my own spine was broken.

It felt like my body had abandoned me, and beneath the physical breakdown, something even more terrifying: I had no idea what was going on in my own mind. I had lost sight of my purpose.

Helping people had never just been a job for me; it was my calling. It brought meaning, connection, and fulfillment. But now, in the stillness of winter, post-surgery, stripped of my role and routine, I felt empty, useless, purposeless, and that, more than the pain, scared me.

That's when the real healing began. Not just of the body but of the deeper wounds I had never fully faced.

In my studies, I had learned that the spine represents more than strength, stability, and flexibility. It holds our history, our structure, and our sense of groundedness. I had none of those.

My injuries weren't random. They were rooted in something deeper. The spine, this sacred channel, was reflecting back years of overextension, of carrying too much, of holding it all together for everyone else.

It was time to stop pushing. It was time to listen and reflect. To finally tend to the trauma I'd buried beneath a life of helping, fixing, striving, and moving too fast for too long. This wasn't just a healing of the spine; it was a healing of oneself.

Looking back, as a child, I was born carrying weight far heavier than I could understand. The responsibilities of the world seemed imprinted into my very tissue. I was both hyper-aware and utterly unsure, sensitive to everything, and yet unable to make sense of what and how I felt.

Intuition pulsed through me, but I didn't know how to hold it. I moved through my early years absorbing the emotions and energy of everyone around me. If someone nearby felt sadness, I felt it deeper. If there was guilt, I carried it as my own. I fretted endlessly about people, about moments, and about things far beyond my control.

Somewhere in that emotional overload, I began developing quiet coping mechanisms. Ways to shoulder the invisible weights around me. As a child my world was small. My home, family, and school were very tight-knit, but the burdens I carried felt massive.

My brother, though seven years older than me, went to the same little church school as I did. My sister, just 18 months younger, was always nearby. That tiny schoolhouse became a sanctuary to me. I felt known, seen, and protected. I remember feeling held by that space, like its walls whispered, "You're safe here."

Everything shifted in the third grade. I was pulled from my warm, familiar school where the message was "Jesus loves you" and began going to the local public school where the message seemed to be the opposite. In that little blue classroom, I suddenly became the outsider. The one they all pointed at.

The safety I once knew vanished. Though I couldn't explain it at the time, I now believe those other children could sense my sensitivity, my openness, my emotional awareness, and it unsettled them. They didn't know what to do with someone who could feel them so clearly. They protected themselves the only way they knew how: through cruelty.

Bullies aren't born mean. They're made from fear, from pain, from homes where love is conditional or absent. When they see someone who can absorb pain without lashing out, they project their own wounds. Because it's easier to hate the mirror than to look into it. I didn't have those words back then. I just knew that the world no longer felt safe. I began to internalize not only their dislike but a growing belief that maybe, just maybe, something was wrong with me.

School was already a challenge for me. I struggled quietly with dyslexia and ADHD, trying to keep up in a world that didn't feel built for the way my brain worked. While others seemed to move through class with ease, I had to fight for every word, every focus, every step of understanding. The one thing I could control was how I showed up at home. I made it my mission to be the easiest child I could be. My siblings were both dealing with depression, and I saw how much it weighed on my mother. I didn't want to add to her burden. So I stayed quiet. I never told her how hard school was, how much it hurt to be teased or misunderstood. I kept it inside. I followed every rule. I made myself small. I thought if I could just stay out of the way, if I could just keep everyone happy, then things would be okay.

It's strange how, as children, we instinctively adapt to survive. I chose to become invisible, not because I lacked value, but because I sensed discomfort and tried to soften it for everyone else. These patterns of self-sacrifice and silence didn't start with me.

This is where my healing journey began to reveal something deeper: these weren't just my patterns, they were inherited. Passed down in ways both spoken and unspoken. I wasn't only responding to my immediate world. I was echoing generations before me.

The need to stay small, the urge to please, and the silence in the face of pain. These intuitions weren't new; they were learned. Embedded in the lineage I came from. Healing, I've come to understand, isn't always just personal. Sometimes, it's ancestral.

To truly know who you are and how you became that person, you have to be willing to look back. Not everyone is. But for those of us who feel stuck, lost, or uncertain, as I did, the past can hold powerful answers.

What shaped us doesn't begin and end with us. Our ancestors' experiences, their traumas, and their survival strategies. They live in us, whether we want them to or not, and healing means honoring that.

To move forward, I had to turn around. I had to acknowledge the pain behind me, the stories, the sacrifices, the silent struggles and decide which parts I wanted to carry forward and which parts I was finally ready to let go.

I grew up in a family where silence was a kind of safety net, where speaking out of turn was quietly frowned upon, and emotions were something you swallowed whole. Truths lived in shadows, tucked neatly into the corners of rooms and hearts. Every woman in my lineage has, in one way or another, been taught the same lessons: Be quiet. Don't cry. Don't be difficult. Don't dream too wildly. Don't speak too loudly, and if you must speak, hurry up and get it out. They came from generations of women who were surviving more than living. Women who learned that silence was safer, self-sacrifice was strength, and it was never delivered in a harsh way. It came wrapped in practicality, in gentle sighs, and weary looks. It was the kind of subtle inheritance that doesn't shout but quietly shapes you. "Be realistic" was the mantra. This is the legacy I come from—strong women who bore too much and asked for too little—but something has been shifting. This is where my story is beginning to diverge.

When I was in high school, everything began to shift, and the ground beneath me felt less and less steady. My grandfather passed away quietly, without a funeral. No gathering, no shared mourning, just silence where closure should have been. A chapter closed without anyone turning the page. Just a phone call in the middle of the night.

Not long after, my cousin passed too. Another loss, layered on top of the first. It felt like grief was becoming part of the background noise of my life, unspoken, unprocessed, and heavy.

Around the same time, my brother left home, forging his own way into the world. I didn't fully understand it then, but his absence left a hole that felt bigger than just the space he previously occupied.

Losing close family members at a young age shapes you in ways you don't fully understand until much later. When death arrives early in your life, it brings with it not just grief but confusion, silence, and unanswered questions. When there are no funerals, no goodbyes, and no rituals of closure, it leaves a particular kind of emptiness. Like a door slammed shut before you even knew someone was leaving.

As a child, I did not have the words for what was happening, but my body remembers. The absence, the shift in energy when I already felt too much. Grief wasn't something to be shared, but something to be managed or hidden. I think none of us knew how to handle grief.

Then my sister moved out, before even graduating high school. Suddenly, I was the only one left at home. The middle child turned into an only child.

The house got quieter, but my mind got louder. I felt abandoned and alone, carrying grief without ritual, transitions without explanation, and a growing sense that everything familiar was slipping away. This season of my life taught me how loss can come in many forms—through death, through distance, and through silence. How the absence of acknowledgment can sometimes hurt just as much as the loss itself.

As the middle child, I had spent my life navigating in-between, never quite the oldest, never quite the youngest. But now, there was no one to balance between. No one to anchor me in our shared chaos. Their leaving left more than just a quiet home. It left a space inside me that I didn't yet know how to fill.

There are two tales woven together here: the one I inherited and the one I am writing. I'm learning to honor the women who came before me without repeating their silence. I'm giving myself permission to live for me. To speak, feel, dream, and expand beyond the edges they were told to stay within and yet, I'm not abandoning the part of me that gives. Helping others is still my calling, but no longer at the cost of abandoning myself.

Some go through life without feeling much at all. They keep moving forward, grinding, pushing in the direction they were told was "success," never stopping long enough to feel the cost of it all. Then, there are those of us who feel everything, who carry the memories of our ancestors not just in dreams, but in our bodies and in our tissue. This right here was imprinted on me before I ever left the womb.

We are the ones who sometimes drift through life feeling a little unmoored, not quite whole, like something ancient is still unfinished within us. We are the empaths, the caregivers, and the healers. We move toward others in service, often to our own detriment. We sense the grief that hasn't been named, the trauma that hasn't been healed.

I adapted to moving faster than I was comfortable, thrived in challenges and other people's problems. Maybe that's what all my injuries and surgeries have really been about. Not just physical healing but spiritual repair. The unraveling of a lineage that is done being quiet. The breaking of patterns that no longer serve.

I've come to believe that the healing I do for myself is not just for me. It's for the women who came before me, who couldn't. It's for my children who follow me.

About Amanda Millay Normand

Amanda Millay Normand is a Kinesiologist, Pilates Teacher, Sports Performance Specialist, and Yoga Teacher who has dedicated her life to helping others discover strength, balance, and resilience through movement. With decades of experience, she has guided people of all ages and abilities to move with greater freedom, confidence, and connection.

Her own healing journey became her greatest teacher. Learning to slow down, listen, and move with intention, Amanda discovered that true transformation is rooted not only in discipline and strength, but also in rest, reflection, and compassion. She finds inspiration in the natural world—walking among the trees, breathing with the ocean, and grounding herself in the quiet wisdom of the earth.

A wife and mother of two boys, Amanda brings the same devotion she has for her family into her work and writing. In *The Power Within Healing*, she shares her personal story of resilience and renewal, hoping to inspire others to honor their bodies, trust their journeys, and uncover the healing power within us all.

Contact or Follow Amanda at:

Email: znormand@gmail.com
Social: @amandaznormand

Stepping Into Center Stage

Caitlin Mahon

I can vividly recall the times in my life when I was lit up from the inside out, and it usually involved dancing and singing, and the prospect of acting someday. I would dance and sing when I was being given permission within a safe space to express myself, like choir and band practices and dance classes, and eventually on stage, even if expressing myself in that safe space felt really scary at the time. But I always had a way of stretching outside my comfort zone, and the fear of not doing it always seemed to be greater than the fear of trying. Something inside of me always knew that THIS is what I am meant to be doing in this lifetime. Expressing myself authentically and with integrity. Yes, on stages, but also in my life—and helping others to do the same.

My path to creating Sing and Sway, a safe space for self-expression through karaoke and dance, has been a long, winding road that continues to unfold before me, with plans to fold breathwork and meditation into what we do. Our offerings are encouraging and inclusive. We create environments where people feel comfortable and confident to explore their own expression, whether it's singing at karaoke or learning the basic steps of ballroom and Latin dance. For the sake of expressing oneself, and not for what it looks or sounds like; meeting you where you are and doing it together. It matters greatly that you use your voice and move your body, and it doesn't matter what it looks or sounds like. This is not *The Voice* nor is it *Dancing with the Stars*, where they have the most elite trainers and celebrity contestants. This is about using movement and music as medicine and helping you take center stage through the seasons of YOUR life. Not to perform for anyone, but to connect with yourself and those around you in your fullest expression. Feeling more comfortable and confident in your own body to express yourself . . . on the microphone, on the dance floor, and in your everyday life.

I. My Story and a Homecoming for My Soul

When I was about five years old, I remember twirling around and playing make believe and saying out loud for the first time ever, "When I grow up, I am going to be a famous artist!" The older child I was playing with laughed and mocked me, saying I would become a "starving artist," a fate that sounded so horrible that I pivoted to the other big dream of mine and said, "Well, then I'll be a famous actress!" In an increasingly mocking tone, she said I "would be a starving actress." It's the earliest memory of countless times that I was bullied growing up, and it felt like her words had power over me. It's not so much what she said to me that mattered. What does matter here is the fact that, like a sponge, my young mind soaked it in as my truth, which kept me stuck and playing small for so long. Sliding door moments in life where I can't help but look back and wonder . . . if those words hadn't been said to me; if I had someone else in the room who had heard what was said and told me differently; if I wasn't often criticized, ridiculed, judged, shamed when I did try to take up space . . . how different would this journey have been for me? I know it's best to *not* think that way because that would mean that I wouldn't have had my own artist's journey that I am still traversing, which makes what I've overcome that much sweeter. But that experience was the beginning of me slowly becoming my own bully and being afraid to be seen and heard, as I was often made to feel small and unworthy when I expressed myself. Not realizing that expressing myself and holding space for others to do the same was my own superpower in the making.

My mom and dad took me to see my older sister's first dance recital around that same age. I was in awe of the glistening costumes, the smell of flowers and hairspray filling the air, the bright lights illuminating the bigness of the stage, the energy in the auditorium as we settled into our seats. When the senior jazz class energetically danced onto stage to "Footloose," dressed in neon pink and green costumes trimmed in black, something inside of me lit up like a bright, shining star from within. Looking up at my mom, I exclaimed, "MOM! I want to do THAT! THAT dance, in THAT costume, to THAT song next year!" How adorable as a little girl that I didn't yet understand how choreographers often create new routines with different music and costumes each year, but all that really mattered in that moment was that I *knew* with every fiber of my being: I am meant to be on stage. As if my soul had whispered to me, "YES! *And* you are meant to be taking center stage, playing the leading lady, with standing ovations. In so. Many. Ways."

But for a little girl who was then consistently bullied and put down in her most formative years, I ended up becoming a painfully shy toddler, tween, and teen, afraid to speak up and use my voice, to take up space, to be seen and heard—without permission and without fear of being rejected or made to feel wrong. I would often feel stuck in my throat, almost like I couldn't speak up and say what was happening to me. So I often remained silent, especially in group settings, and I figured out ways to express myself that didn't require words.

* * *

At a young age, my parents thankfully put my sister and me in dance classes, and my dad taught us how to ski. Two activities that grew my self-esteem, which I continued until an unexpected, abrupt end in my early 30s (more on that later). Taking classes in ballet, jazz, lyrical, pointe, tap, modern, and musical theater shaped and molded me into the woman I am. Ski trips and dance classes served as outlets when it felt like I couldn't access my voice.

Dance class became a place where I could go within and connect with myself. Moving my body as a dancer was helping me process much of what I couldn't express with my voice, but on a somatic level. It felt like breathing, like a safe haven, like an old, reliable friend, and a home I would always be able to return to. Feeling safer in performing on stage, where I was in the same costume, doing the same movements as my classmates. Not singled out, and not in center stage.

Outside of dancing, skiing, band, and choir, I was a creative, multi-passionate girl. The overachiever in me thought her self-worth was found in productivity. An Honor student. Varsity athlete in track and field hockey. A youth group leader. A volunteer for most school clubs. The list goes on. And all the while, I was dreaming of acting, yet never going for it.

* * *

I had a reading problem in kindergarten that required help from a reading specialist. Even though I became a strong reader and eventually a professional journalist, I dreaded being called on in class to read out loud during my K–12 education. My face would turn red, my body would get hot, my stomach would twist and turn into knots, and I would want to run. Classmates would sometimes make fun of me for mispronouncing a word or for reading more slowly than other students.

In elementary school, skiing and dancing continued, and I naturally gravitated toward choir and band. But by 6th grade, my school district's restructuring of schools landed me in a classroom where I only knew *one* out of 30+ students. I was badly bullied by classmates and eventually by my own teacher.

That year, my 21-year-old babysitter and my beloved grandfather passed away within two days of each other. My mom lost her father and favorite person in the world, and I was doing my best to survive life in the 6th grade without making my parents' lives more difficult. Turning within and suffering in silence. As the school's holiday choir concert approached, I was considering giving up band *and* choir, thinking that would be two less things to bully me about, and because I was increasingly *not* okay. I remember trying to make myself invisible with hunched-over shoulders, barely opening my mouth to halfheartedly sing, all the while wishing for Christmas break to begin already. I knew I was being made fun of by classmates, but I never thought it would be my own teacher, too.

After the concert, my teacher humiliated me in front of the

entire class, saying that she didn't know why I was up there, noting how I barely opened my mouth to sing. Turning beet red, my entire body felt like it was being tied up in knots. The entire class laughed at me. I abruptly quit band and choir, running away from part of what I was *meant* to do in this life.

I always had friends growing up, but bullies seemed to be found in most places. Not to mention the internalized bully and critic within me, who was growing louder. I remember how moments like that would take major hits at my self-esteem and worthiness, and make me want to shrivel up into nothing, and just disappear.

Despite the acting dream alive within my heart and soul, it didn't exactly feel safe to read lines and sing solo in front of anyone at an audition, let alone in a musical on stage. So I never really tried, even as that dream inside of me only continued to grow.

* * *

In preparing for college, I strongly desired to go for dance education, yet lacked the confidence to try, and my parents preferred that I majored in something that would afford more job security. Writing had become a passion as I joined my high school newspaper. As a student at Rutgers University in New Brunswick, I graduated with a Bachelor of Science in Exercise Science and a double major in Journalism, interned with *Good Housekeeping* magazine and the New Jersey Nets, and worked my way up the editorial board at *The Daily Targum*, the Rutgers student newspaper. I didn't stop dancing either, serving as a choreographer and performer for Rutgers Performing Dance Company.

I also couldn't *not* sing, especially the music of my favorite singer-songwriter, Sara Bareilles. It was Sara's music that helped me find my "little voice," singing alone where no one could hear me, matching pitch with Sara, who felt like a soul sister holding space for me to explore my self-expression. (Side-note: I later had the privilege of meeting Sara at her book signing!) This incredible woman's music has been part of my life since 2007, helping me navigate heartbreak and heartache alike, from relationships to my car accident, injuries, and chronic pain journey, and making me feel like I'm not alone. This hasn't changed, either.

After graduating in 2010, despite the burning desire to act, sing, and dance professionally growing within me, I was working as an editor for two Patch.com websites for three years in Union County, NJ. A freak skiing accident in 2013 was my wake-up call to start pursuing dance again, so I left my journalism career, picked up freelancing and a side hustle with ARBONNE International (where I overcame my fear of public speaking), and returned to my hometown dance studio as a competitive dancer and assistant instructor. That was my life for several years, while dabbling in banking and advertising careers. I remember being happy to be dancing again, yet wanting more *and* knowing I was capable of much more in the performing arts.

* * *

Getting my heart broken when I was 30 years old, a month after we were shopping for engagement rings, wasn't in my life plan. I thought we were in love, creating a life together, while he was creating his exit strategy. At nearly nine years older than me and divorced, I thought he was somehow different from other guys I had dated. As I sat in his living room in my robe one morning, messy hair thrown up in a bun, eating a reheated frittata from the day before, he said we should see other people. After 7+ years together.

It was one of the few times in life when I felt like the world was crashing down all around me. It didn't take long for my intuition to pick up on the fact that there *was* another woman, and after much probing, he finally admitted to his "emotional affair" with his coworker, as if having an emotional affair was somehow *not* the same as a physical affair? I gave my power away as I asked him to stay with me and try to make it work, and to stop talking to her while we did. Upon arrival at a previously planned ski trip, I asked him to confirm if he had stopped talking to her. The whole car ride, my intuition had been confirming for me that he still was, and that this wasn't going to work. My intuition has never lied to me.

Moving back home at 30, I was filled with an ocean of confusing feelings and emotions bumping up against everything and everyone else in my life. I had this false subconscious belief that I was supposed to be engaged or married by 30, and that because I wasn't, there was something wrong with me. Clearly, I thought, I'm not enough or worthy or deserving, not yet having the awareness that my inherent self-worth comes from within. Watching as most women around my age were getting engaged, getting married, having babies, buying their dream homes, and so on. I was tied up in that false narrative for longer than I care to admit and have been working to disentangle myself from it, layer by layer. After all, it's just a construct of patriarchy that women feel they need to get married and have babies in the first place, that it's not socially acceptable to propose to your partner or have a baby alone, and that it means something about their worth if they don't by a certain age, or in the "right" way, or at all. I call it bullshit.

I felt like a hollowed-out shell of the energetic, creative, driven woman I was before. But that time allowed me to come back to my center and collect the pieces of myself—yes, I was heartbroken, but I was also opening myself up to new people, places, and experiences for the first time in my post-college life. Around this time, I trained in ballroom and Latin dance. I didn't know at the time how these experiences would later serve as the partial foundation for my business, Sing and Sway.

In 2018, after a year of training and with encouragement from friends, I began hosting beginner social dancing events in public venues. This was in part because I realized two things. A lot of people are intimidated by ANY dance studio environment, and a more casual setting may do the trick. And while the best way to learn is by rotating partners, not everyone wants to learn that way, and many are looking for additional learning formats. So I began offering beginner social dancing lessons in less intimidating environments, where transitioning partners was optional.

That same year, I met John—the love of my life and my dance partner—who is now my fiancé.

Sing and Sway was officially founded in 2019, and we were rocking and rolling with dance offerings, and launching karaoke. But 2020 had other plans. The world shut down as a global pandemic raged, and my family and I lost Alex and Emma, our beloved 13-year-old rescue dogs, two months apart. If that wasn't enough, my life reached an inflection point and would never be the same again.

A car accident left me with a permanently injured lower back and triggered symptoms of a serious neurological condition I never knew I had, known as Chiari Malformation Type 1.

This accident and my injuries completely altered my life. It forced me to take time off from growing Sing and Sway for a while, and continues to inform and impact my ability to expand and grow. While I'm able to teach a limited amount of basic ballroom and Latin dance, helping people to feel comfortable and confident, my hopes of dancing in the way I was able to for most of my life were dashed in the blink of an eye.

Chiari malformation is a serious neurological condition where your brain descends into your spinal column, pressing on your brain stem and blocking proper cerebral spinal fluid flow. There is no cure, and there are no guarantees from decompression surgery. My daily life since my 2020 car accident has been the most challenging—a chronic state of survival mode, a never-ending rollercoaster ride of chronic pain, research and education, doctor appointments, insurance, out-of-state opinions from Chiari specialists, grieving what my body can no longer do, advocating for myself, missing out on a lot, and explaining to people what I am able and not able to do. It doesn't help that there is little understanding about Chiari malformation within the medical community and even less so among the general public.

As someone who has been a lifelong overachiever, burning the candle at both ends, as well as being a varsity athlete, an expert skier, and a seasoned dancer for most of her life, my accident and diagnosis completely changed everything. I went into a familiar pattern where I didn't want to burden or add to anyone's plate, especially amid a global pandemic. Everyone was going through so much, with people losing loved ones, homes, jobs, and more, and I was repeating patterns from childhood where I was shutting down and operating from a functional freeze state, only opening up to my doctors and a select number of loved ones.

Living with an invisible illness like Chiari malformation shifts your perspective in life where you begin approaching others with more kindness. Yes, I still get this wrong sometimes as a human being, but I remind myself every day that a lot of people are fighting battles that I know little to nothing about, whether it's physical, mental, emotional, or a combination. We are more connected than ever, yet so disconnected beyond the surface level. It's easier for people to mask and say "I'm okay" when they are not. Just because you can't see it doesn't mean their pain and suffering aren't real and impacting their daily life. Oftentimes, I've found that by being brave enough to say, "I'm not okay," and vulnerably sharing what happened and is happening instead of masking or pretending everything is okay, is incredibly healing and expansive for both parties. Opening up gives your loved one permission to take the brave step of saying, "I'm not okay, too," and this is why, and this is what happened and is happening to me. We are meant to be healing in community, not alone.

I didn't ask for any of this: the car accident, the permanent back injury, the Chiari malformation diagnosis, the progressive symptoms, the brain surgery, the potential for more brain surgery, the laundry list of symptoms that I live with daily, the impact on every aspect of my life, the uncertainty about how the hell I am going to be able to take care of myself for the rest of my life, the delay of getting married and having babies and the can of worms that would come with becoming a mother, the potential to pass this onto my child, how I struggle to take care of myself from day to day, so how would I be able to raise a child? Children need to be lifted and held, and all of the things that will likely trigger and flare up symptoms. Carrying even 5–10 pounds and repeated arm movements and gripping of items make my pain worse, and may trigger a Chiari malformation headache that will force me to lie down with ice and medicine. The medical bills and financial strain this has placed on my life, my significant other, and my parents. The navigation of insurance, and only getting the answers I needed to obtain the insanely expensive insurance plan at the final hour in 2022 that would allow me to go out-of-state, so that I would be able to move forward with my scheduled Chiari malformation decompression surgery in February 2023.

I didn't sign up for this: having to give up dancing and skiing in the way my body was used to dancing and skiing for most of my life. Even having to give up favorite pastimes, like fishing, bowling, and riding rollercoasters. Giving up any hope of weight training, or even a yoga or pilates class without massive modifications. It's heartbreaking. Having so much that I want to do in my life, yet having little physical capacity for most of it. Saying no or canceling plans because my body is in too much pain. The impact on my loved ones . . . I may be the one who has all these crazy symptoms, who had the brain surgery and may need more brain surgery, but my support system went through it, too.

Before and certainly after my surgery, it became clear that I could not sustain working a day job while living with a lifelong, painful neurological condition with no cure, especially at a job where they weren't promoting me despite my best efforts. I was already on a spiritual healing journey that had been kick-started after my heartbreak at 30, with my dear friend, Dana Garced, which was life-changing. Working with Dana allowed me to learn meditation and reflection practices, establish boundaries and align energetically with the seasons, and access greater awareness and healing of subconscious beliefs and narratives.

When the opportunity came up to begin working with Nicole Smith Levay, it was a resounding YES from my intuition and my body. Almost as if there was a great threshold before me where I was being guided by my intuition to leap. My body, soul, and energy began to shift even more as I was guided through meditation and breathwork practices and Nicole's life-changing Forward Momentum program. I was coming home to myself even more, setting clearer boundaries and putting my needs first, treating myself like my own best friend, and doing my best to care for myself every day. Listening to my intuition on a new level. Learning to trust myself more, and reminding myself that I can get through anything, even if it doesn't feel that way. My resilience has been greatly tested and may as well be my middle name now, but I keep getting back up every time I'm knocked down. I continue to tell myself that I can see this through, and there is light ahead for me, and there is a way through the chronic pain. Doing my best to reframe any doubts, fears, or false narratives in real time, which is no easy feat. But as

Glennon Doyle so eloquently wrote in her book *Untamed*, "We Can Do Hard Things." YES, *we can do hard things.*

II. Stepping Into My Center Stage

In the Hollywood version of my story, they would find a cure for Chiari malformation and herniated discs, I would somehow overcome it all, and go on to become the Broadway triple threat I always dreamed I'd be. Yet there is no cure, I'm not able to dance anymore beyond the basic steps that I teach, I'm not a Broadway star, and my pain dictates what I'm able to do from day to day. Instead, I have been on a spiritual journey unfolding before me, where I have stripped back the false stories that I was told about myself, including what I told myself about me. I learned to love myself and to become my own best friend. And as any best friend would, after the hell I've been through and continue to endure, I decided it was high time to finally stop playing small, step out of the shadows, and into the center stage of my dreams. In whatever accessible and accommodating ways I am able. Because if not now, *when*? Someday, the curtain will fall on my life. There is *no* dress rehearsal . . . this is it!

I eventually made my debut on stage, singing solo at a local community cabaret. As my confidence continued to grow, I auditioned for community singing and acting opportunities that were accommodating, accessible, and aligned for me, including a local paid cabaret in which I was cast. Our rehearsal process ignited a newfound belief within myself that *yes*, acting and singing professionally *may* be possible for me after all. Not only was I afforded a professional opportunity to sing but also the chance to share my story on stage for the first time. The stage, a microphone, the audience, my voice, and my truth. Was it Broadway? No, but it sure felt like it to my inner child, beaming with joy, with a bright spotlight shining on me, the quiet, supportive presence of the audience, my body, soul, and energy taking center stage, and my truth and voice filling up every corner and crevice. Being seen, heard, and witnessed in my authentic, embodied expression. It was one of the most healing and cathartic experiences, one that I will be forever grateful for, where I felt *safe* to be seen and heard in my truth for the first time, which has given me the courage to begin pursuing acting and singing professionally, and more courage to continue sharing my story, including in this anthology.

Fittingly, I chose to sing "She Used to Be Mine" from the musical *Waitress*, with music and lyrics by my musical hero, Sara Bareilles. Those many years of solo cathartic singing experiences with Sara's music led to this opportunity, where I was held in this beautiful, safe space to say and sing my truth, out loud.

> *. . . I have found my voice, the one I was so afraid to express for most of my life, and I'm going to keep using it. And for now, I can use my voice to say this: I am going after my dream of singing and acting professionally. It is never too late to pursue your dreams. As for each past version of me? I know in my soul that she did the best she could with what she knew at the time, and* ***she used to be mine.***

I chose to move through my pain, and I make that choice again and again, every day. What else is there to do? I choose to move forward. Even when it hurts, even while my body is screaming every day in pain. I choose to keep putting one foot in front of the other, even when I'm dismissed, or when someone misunderstands what I am going through, or when pain management says they've done all they can for me. I keep moving forward, even when the MRI scans show I may need more surgery. I keep moving forward, even when the world is in chaos. We are not what happens to us. Those experiences do not define us. Yet how we move through it and what we tell ourselves and who we become and unbecome in that process . . . that's what *matters*. Keep moving forward, even when it hurts so damn much. Even when there's no end to the chaos and pain in sight. Keep. Moving. Forward.

We are meant to follow our dreams and what lights us up inside. We are meant to be stepping into our own center stage. Imagine if we all did that, what a world this would be. I know that by not stepping into my center stage, I wouldn't be fulfilling my soul purpose, which is still unfolding before me, with people along my path that will be impacted by my story, whom I haven't met yet, shining a bright light on my pain and using it to purposefully help others through their own. I know that by not stepping into my center stage, I wouldn't be reaching the people I am meant to reach. And so, while I can't see the path ahead, I trust and have faith that I am being divinely led, and so are you. You wouldn't be reading this story right now if you weren't. Keep. Moving. Forward.

III. Stepping Into Your Center Stage

By not stepping into *your* Center Stage, what would that *mean* for you and your life? Most of us are so afraid that we're not enough, and because we're not enough, we won't be loved. And when we don't feel that we are good enough or loved, we may not step into center stage in our own lives.

It took me a long time to realize that I had been cast as the main character of my life. Perhaps you're realizing now that you, too, have been cast as the main character in your life. Even if you did already know this, do you act like it? Many of us are unaware that we are sitting on the sidelines, playing the role of the supporting character rather than the star of our story. Putting our worthiness in the hands of another person, place, opinion, situation, job, or experience.

I've learned there are people walking this Earth who will make you feel like you ARE enough and that you ARE loved. Yet what is profoundly more important and serves as the basis for all of your relationships, is that you make yourself feel like you ARE enough and that you ARE loved. It only makes you more resilient and better prepared to navigate the journey ahead, especially when in contact with people and places and experiences that make you feel unloved or like you're not enough, yet you know the truth, and act from that place instead.

We are all inherently worthy and loved by this dear Universe, all on our own, and we deserve the life of our dreams. We simply need to give ourselves permission . . . to step into the leading role of our lives, and take Center Stage.

I invite you to ask yourself, "What is *my* center stage?" It may be releasing what people said wasn't possible for you. For some, it may be an actual stage like mine, with someone saying no, you can't go after your dream, or you're not good enough. But in other ways, it could be that you were made to feel like you need to shrink or change to fit in, someone saying your dreams aren't possible for you, someone telling you to stay in this or that box. Maybe it's taking control of your life, setting boundaries, having difficult conversations, starting that business with your passion and leaving the soul-sucking job, or fill in the blank. Perhaps it's trying something new, like taking a dance class, or singing at karaoke, or auditioning for a local cabaret. Maybe it's going back to what you loved to do as a kid. Maybe it's applying for that dream job before you feel ready. Maybe it's going back to identifying and building awareness around the subconscious beliefs that were planted in the roots of your being and rewriting the story from there. You're the director and the star, and it's your story. You can always rewrite what happens for you next.

What do you need to release and let go of to make space to take *your* center stage? If your life were a movie right now, what would the audience be screaming at the screen for you to do next? If you met yourself at 90 years old, what would you tell yourself? Tomorrow is *not* guaranteed. Age is not a stop sign, but a big shiny green light that says, "You're alive! Let's go, baby! Go for it! If not now, *when*?! Take the leap! YES, you *can*!" I thought my life was over at 30, and again at 33. It was anything but.

As Lin-Manuel Miranda sings in *Hamilton*, one of my favorite musicals, "It's time to take a shot, and I am not throwing away my shot." It's time to take *your* shot! I'm taking mine, in whatever accessible and accommodating way I am able, with singing and acting, amidst the chaos and chronic pain. I am leaping into the unknown, with a lot of support from my loving fiancé, my dear parents, and loved ones, and we can do this together. It's time to go for it and take your Center Stage. Even if it hurts, even if people don't understand or make fun of you or judge you. At the end of your life, the opinions of other people won't matter, but what you chose to do in spite of anyone else's opinions, and what you chose to do with your time on this Earth, will be all that matters.

It's safe to express yourself. It's never too late to connect with your inner wisdom, and step into your innate desires and dreams. And it doesn't need to be a journey kick-started with a traumatic medical marathon that you didn't sign up for. It may be as simple as you reading this story and reflecting on what is moving within you right now. Do you need someone to tell you to go for it? Here I am, sharing that I *believe* that you can *and* you will! You need to believe it, too, and please, borrow my belief as needed as you grow yours within . . . because YES, YOU CAN! What's even better is knowing this is not merely a destination, but a journey, one that is much better taken in a supportive community. You are not alone, and we can do this together . . . as you take *your* Center Stage.

* * *

Along this journey, my center stage continues to move and shift just as I do—and it may for you, too. At times, I feel myself slipping back into the familiar, safe, comfortable sidelines, where it's easier to not uphold that boundary or not have the difficult conversation or not to audition. Backstage or off stage, literally and figuratively, when I am meant to be *shining brightly* in center stage. I feel this all the more as I live with Chiari malformation and chronic pain. Yet as my own best friend, I'm learning to gently, playfully nudge myself back into the spotlight and to adjust my crown while I'm at it. Honoring my intuition, boundaries and pain, and what my body needs from day to day. Remembering that I am worthy and more than enough for myself. Always have been. Always will be. Without needing to be accepted or understood. Expressing myself because I can and I want to, and it makes me feel the most aligned. Seen. Heard. Witnessed. Lit up from within. In *My* Center Stage.

About Caitlin Mahon

Caitlin Mahon is a professional actor and vocalist, former competitive dancer, and owner of Sing and Sway, which fosters safe space for self-expression through karaoke, dance, breathwork, and meditation.

With a passion for and strong foundation in dancing and performing that was nurtured in childhood at Dance with Marie, Caitlin had opportunities to participate in regional and national competitions, perform in Walt Disney World, and train with the Radio City Rockettes. At Rutgers University-New Brunswick, Caitlin served as a choreographer and performer with Rutgers Performing Dance Company. Earning a B.S. in Exercise Science (Sports Management), Caitlin double-majored in Journalism, leading her to AOL/Patch as a professional editor and reporter.

After a 2013 skiing accident, Caitlin's path led back to Dance with Marie as a competitive dancer and assistant instructor. Her entrepreneurial spirit led Caitlin to create Sing and Sway in 2019, offering inclusive beginner ballroom and Latin dance classes, private wedding dance lessons, and karaoke events.

A 2020 car accident ended Caitlin's lifelong dance career, permanently injuring her back and leading to brain surgery in 2023 due to triggered Chiari Malformation symptoms. Amid her ongoing chronic pain journey, Caitlin aspires to raise awareness of invisible illnesses, and inspire others to take Center Stage in their own lives.

Follow Caitlin on Instagram @singandsway or connect at singandsway.com.

YOU STAY . . . I GO . . .
No Following

Secret Offerings and Teachings from
My Soulful Daughter

Cinzia Marie

To my beloved daughter, Amanda:

Long before this lifetime, your soul and mine touched hands and hearts in mystery. You looked into the future and chose me, and in that choice, you carried wisdom far beyond this world. You came before me, and you returned for me and now through me to bring forth and guide me in your enlightened ways. You lived with fearless light venturing into realms only the courageous dare explore. I now carry the voice with which you came, and the voice with which you went, sharing it with those willing to step into the unchartered chambers of their own being, waiting to awaken.

"There is no coming to consciousness without pain. People will do anything, no matter how absurd, to

avoid facing their own soul. Yet whoever looks within awakens to eternity."

—Carl Jung

With deep humility and spiritual clarity, I offer this unfolding path—a mother's journey through the unthinkable and into something holy: a presence that lives beyond the veil. Amanda is not felt here as someone who left, but as someone who expanded—became the light in every corner, whispers in every wind, truth in every moment I dare to be still, even across realms.

And they were stars under her feet as she danced to the songs of her heart . . .
And the sound of the waves under dark lit sky
No moon to be seen
Just the stars beneath her feet
She Danced

—Amanda Hills

My voice, once shaped in courtrooms transcribing human truth, is now shaped by something older, something timeless. I speak as a mother, as a healer, as one who has walked through fire and emerged glowing with embers of eternity.

This writing honors many spiritual paths, offering an open doorway into the universal truth: our love is eternal, and souls never die. Deep within me, filtered through a multi-spiritual lens, I share my newfound knowledge that as we evolve spiritually, we gain the ability to access higher dimensions within ourselves, realms of existence that offer broader perspective and understanding of the universe and our place within it. We are all awakening—through love, through grace, through purpose—guided across lifetimes by something greater than ourselves.

And so, I invite you: feel your heart. Close your eyes and let yourself remember what you already know. That healing is not forgetting. It is listening more deeply. It is seeing, not with the eyes, but with vision.

"The only thing worse than blindness is having sight without the ability to see."

Originally believed to be of Helen Keller. Whether she spoke it or not, the truth remains eternal.

* * *

It had been 36 hours since I last saw her. Then—the knock on the door. Before I even opened it, I felt the heaviness and immediately knew once I opened that door that my life was going to change forever. Standing before me were three individuals whom I recognized as plain-clothed detectives whose faces carried the weight of the news that no parent should ever have to hear. It could only mean one thing. Without any words, I knew. She was gone.

I fell to the ground, screeching at the top of my lungs, noises that I didn't know the body could make. Gasping for air while at the same time, hoping it would be my last so that I could be with her. What followed was an unimaginable blur that lasted a prolonged period of time, which seemed like one continuous dark moment to me.

Throughout that time I was offered support, I received letters, books, and teachings in the hopes of helping me navigate through this unimaginable loss. I read each and every one of them when I could focus my eyes clearly enough. The one thought that was ever present in my mind was that I wanted to follow her. At that time I felt as though my purpose on earth was done, and my only child was somewhere beyond where I could see. Where that was, I didn't know.

I was lost in confusion about my faith and my religious beliefs. I didn't understand why our creator would impose such pain, or perhaps sickness, to a young life so full of promise and purpose that she would end her life by her own choosing. I have, through time and teaching, come to understand that her departure was part of something far greater than imaginable.

Amanda didn't just leave. She transcended her being, just as she had planned. I now know with absolute certainty that Amanda knew I would be the one to carry her light forward—to help guide others into greater awareness. She chose me to remind me that I, too, could choose my path. That I could expand my beliefs, softening what I once held tightly, and live a life rooted in trust and certainty—trusting that every experience along the way, even the ones that broke me, were gifts.

> *"The wound is the place where the Light enters you."*
>
> **—Jalal al-Din Rumi**

Each day now, I rise with quiet appreciation for the beauty unfolding before me—sometimes in light, sometimes in ache. I still rise and fall with the rhythm of this human life. I still feel pain; I often shed tears. Only now they're not tears of sadness; they are quite the opposite. When Amanda left, the walls that I had built unconsciously within myself and around me began to crack, collapsing completely. And in their place, I began to rebuild. Not just my beliefs, but my very self—reconstructed with the wisdom that now flows through me. Your voice lives in mine, your wings carrying me through.

* * *

In an underlined passage in one of Amanda's books, the *Bhagavad Gita*, where the ancient Sanskrit speaks of the soul's journey through time:

> *"The self wears the body as a garment; when the garment is old, it is cast aside, and a new one is put on. Just as death is certain for the living, rebirth is certain for the dead."*

It was there I first read the word *Samsara*—not simply meaning rebirth, but the sacred cycle itself. The flow of soul through life after life. Amanda left these pages marked, knowing that I would read them, as if to say: there is no end, only change. No goodbyes, only transformations.

Later in the margins of another page, Amanda had placed a line beneath a sentence that made me pause and reflect:

> *"Evolution, according to the Gita, is a painful, slow return to our native state."*

Reflecting on that with newfound insight, I came to understand that the soul's journey isn't about becoming something new. It's about remembering. Turning inward. Returning to what we've always been. Remembering that wholeness is never truly lost. And perhaps that's why it hurts so deeply—because the path back to our essence asks us to shed all the illusions we've worn for lifetimes.

As days became months, and time stood still while somehow simultaneously passing by at speeds beyond comprehension, I came to realize that grief offers no clear direction. It's not a staircase leading upward. It is a spiral, circling back and forth, pulling us under and lifting us up until we are ready to step away from the patterns that no longer carry us forward.

The way I was moving through the world no longer brought me closer to Amanda. It pulled me deeper into shadows of what once was. It was torturous in its honesty because I now had to ignite a light entirely on my own. One that looked nothing like the life Amanda and I had dreamed of or imagined. Not for her, not for me, not for us.

We often spoke of a future—one where Amanda would continue to serve as a guide, a teacher, a vessel of healing. She had been leading others through the arts of yoga, Pilates, mixed martial arts movement, dance, and literature while providing nourishment to the less fortunate as well as the fortunate.

Soulga, Amanda's vision, held a mission statement so simple and profound: empowering one person at a time to engage mind, body, and spirit. That is without question exactly what she did. I invite you to take a journey to Amanda's Instagram page, Soulga, where each image or post gives you a glimpse into her spirit, the way she saw beauty in ordinary days, and the way she offered herself to others without reservation. You will see a beautiful being devoted to healing and inspiration through the artistry of her yoga practice, the wisdom of her words, and the undeniable spark that touched many lives. Through the story, I know you will feel as I now do, that Amanda's story does not end with her absence, it transformed beyond what my eyes could see, living now deep within me as a truth I feel in my bones. It blooms in connection. It grows in every heart willing to feel and open itself, allowing the whispers, reminding you that we are all part of something timeless and infinite. May you feel her joy. May you feel her peace. And may you carry forward even a small piece of her light into your own journey.

* * *

Amanda and I often shared quiet moments wrapped in stories—simple choices at the time—which now, in my infinite wisdom, I note to be messages that she was trying to share with me from an already knowing, early age. One of her favorite movies was *The Iron Giant*, a story that became our unspoken language. It tells of a mysterious iron giant who crash lands on Earth, lost and uncertain, until a boy named Hogarth sees his soul and offers him new understanding about who he is and what his purpose is. Amanda, too, arrived in this world through a crash.

There is a moment in the film when Hogarth explains to the giant with kindness, "You are who you choose to be." Amanda lived by that truth. She refused to let circumstances define her. She chose courage. She chose love. She chose authenticity—even when life challenged her repeatedly and deeply. The most poignant of the messages and the words that we repeated to each other through the years, while simultaneously pointing to one another, and then the sky: "You stay. I go. No following."

Just as *The Iron Giant* asked Hogarth in the movie, "You . . . die?" *Hogarth*: "Well . . . yes, someday." *The Iron Giant*: "I die?" *Hogarth*: "I don't know. You're made of metal . . . but you have feelings. And you think about things. And that means you have a soul. And souls don't die." *The Iron Giant*: "Soul?" *Hogarth*: "Mom says it's something inside of all good things . . . and that means it goes on forever and ever." *The Iron Giant*: "Souls don't die." Pointing inside to his heart.

I believe Amanda already knew their meaning. She knew she would want to leave before me, after first teaching me to see this world through a different light—one that no book or school could ever teach.

> *"When an entity has become aware of the evolutionary process, it chooses the manner of its life experience in order to maximize the lessons to be learned."*
>
> **—The Law of One**

Three years ago, you left this earth, Amanda—leaving behind the greatest part of you: me. Now imagining how to go on. Grief had taken over my body, my mind, my every move, and my spirit. My memory began to slip. My body ached. Injuries and illness came one after another. Hospitalizations blurred into each other. I was making myself sick.

Yet somewhere deep inside, something remained. I surrounded myself with the tribe that you knew would guide me and hold me, kindred spirits, those that had known you, loved you and been marked by your light. Together, we would return to places that you loved, enjoyed your passions. I walked the paths you once walked, hoping that through those adventures I might find you again.

> *"The soul never dies. It is not born. It is eternal, changeless, immortal. Birth and death are but doors through which we pass to gain new experiences."*
>
> **—Paramahansa Yogananda**

* * *

When Amanda arrived at our home in Florida, I didn't yet realize it was to say goodbye—but she did. She had been in an altered state for some time, moving through waves of uncertainty, visiting with friends and family along the entire East Coast. Each visit, she knew, would be her last. There was a quiet purpose guiding her. She had made the journey with her devoted companion, Hercules, her dog, her son, her hero, her steady presence through it all.

She came to bring him home. Not just to visit, but to place him where she knew he would be safe, cherished, and protected for the rest of his days. He was 12 years old when he got home. In addition to Amanda, he, too, was drained by the journey. Never leaving her side. She entrusted him to me knowing he would be with his K-9 sister Demi, my loyal service dog, so they could grow old together, surrounded by our love. As I write this, Hercules went on to meet his mom, Amanda, three months ago. My vision is crystal clear; he is her Pegasus, gliding through the skies, reunited and happy again.

She stayed with me for just 16 hours, but in that small span of time, love filled every corner. Amanda moved with intention—gentle, present, luminous. At one point, she stepped into the bathroom while I was showering and quietly sat down, just to be near me and speak to me in a quiet tone. She then began to speak tenderly, truthfully—sharing things she had never said before. I asked her why she was telling me now, and she smiled softly, "Just because I thought you should know." There was no edge, only full transparency in the way she spoke and looked at me that was a clarifying moment for her, and one day become clear for me. Not understood by me at the time. Now fully processed as I ascended in my spirituality, every word relived in our relationship became my teacher. This was the path of guidance knowing one day I would have no more questions.

I remembered how you once gathered others in healing ways—how you held space through your women's retreats, guiding those ready to awaken to the fullness of who they were. When a dear friend suggested I join a retreat in Costa Rica, I said yes, hoping that I would find you in the same way others had once found themselves through you.

Well, deep in the heart of the jungle, I found myself encircled by healers and a beautiful soul family. Our food was prepared with love, carrying a beauty so rich that it felt like a warm embrace, leaving you not just nourished in the body but in the soul. We shared our stories, each leading us to a place where we may find some clarity. My faith had been fractured, my belief system broken. And in that moment, something began to awaken.

* * *

Your favorite color had always been red. In some of your final drawings and works of art, you were presenting images of dragonflies. Your journals filled with words about transformation, transition, metamorphosis.

One afternoon while still on retreat in Costa Rica, my heart too heavy to hold, I looked into the sky and whispered, "If you are with me, baby girl, please show yourself as a red dragonfly."

In moments closely following, a giant red dragonfly swept through the field of my vision, and my heart stopped until you settled on a magnificent tree. There you sat, slowly opening and closing your wings, pausing as if to stop time —giving me a moment to steady my breath and bear witness through the lens, framing your stillness through my tear-filled eyes.

I was told later by the locals when I shared with them the miraculous sighting I had that day, they themselves were taken aback, as they told me that red dragonflies, especially of that size, were rare in that area of Costa Rica. It was at that instant that I knew with clarity that cut through the grief: you never left me. You were there beside me, above me, below me. You are and always will be the wind beneath my wings.

One evening during a meditative sound healing, we were caught in the first great rainstorm of the season. We were in a standalone wood-covered structure open to towering trees and the dark greenness with all of the sounds provided by Mother Nature. The storm roared, branches cracking and breaking around us as our musical journey continued.

It was in that moment—deep in a meditative state, the storm surrounding us—that your voice pierced through, wrapped in love and certainty:

"Straighten your crown, Mama." Then softly you whispered, "Slow down. Just be. You don't have to do anything."

I remember shaking my head in disbelief. "Straighten your crown"—those were words that became a light hearted joke between us. That I had a will that would not bend, and so did she. That I carried a fierce spirit, and she carried it, too. Knowing that she was just as unstoppable. Specifically, I would say to you,

"Straighten your crown. After all, you know whose daughter you are."

Your message was received loud and clear at that moment, once again assuring me that you are right there with me and that you've never gone away.

As I move through life with its ups and downs, as life does, I now hear those words—only they are reversed. Now I hear you say . . . "Straighten your crown, Mama. You know whose mother you are." As your voice drifts off until the next time I need a gentle reminder.

This healing journey opened the doors to healing within me that I might still have doubted had you not shown up at the exact moment that I called for you.

* * *

When you left your earthly body, you wore just one piece of jewelry—a bracelet that I had given you engraved with the Latin words *Alis Volat Propriis*, the meaning of which is . . . She flies by her own wings.

Those words now live etched forever down my spine, giving me strength to rise above all that comes to me knowing that you will always be the wind beneath my wings.

> *"We are all visitors to this time, this place. We are just passing through. Our purpose here is to observe, to learn, to grow."*
>
> **—Aboriginal proverb**

As time passed, my heart could not stop searching for you. I meditated daily; I journaled feverishly night after night trying to capture what feelings were inside of me as well as what I had learned as I learned it. It was then that I sought out paths of every kind. I began studying living religions left in the many books of Amanda which she so deeply followed, which reflected her connection to some part of each, including Hinduism, Buddhism, Judaism,

Christianity. I explored astrological teachings while simultaneously delving into and learning about numerology along with tarot.

I immersed myself in a tapestry of wisdom, drawn from sacred teachings, timeless philosophies, and the insights of philosophers, scientists, and spiritual guides such as The Law of One, A Course in Miracles, the wisdom of Kabbalah, Rumi, Paramahansa Yogananda, the Bhagavad Gita, Bruce Lee, ancient mythologies, and countless others who crossed my path. I traveled to ancient ruins, remote jungles, and secret spaces. I stood in places where the very air itself whispered messages from mystical places unknown.

As my knowledge base had expanded, a gentle shift began to stir within me, a calmness that slowly and delicately filled my mind, my heart, and my entire being. It was then that the words Amanda so often quoted and used in her practice came to my mind, and I remembered the teachings of Bruce Lee.

> *"Be shapeless, formless, like water. When you pour water into a cup, it becomes the cup. When you pour water into a bottle, it becomes a bottle. When you pour water into a teapot, it becomes the teapot. Water can drip, and it can crash. Become like water, my friend."*

* * *

Once the fog of early grief began to lift, I was finally able to see what was there from the start, to hear what had always been calling. I was able to stop focusing of the pain of Amanda's departure and instead focus of the blessings of how she lived her life, in the most authentic way, "DeManda" style.

Red was always Amanda's favorite color. And in many traditions and hearts, the red cardinal carries a sacred message. It is said when a cardinal appears, so does a visitor from the spirit world. These vivid messengers arrive in moments soon after departing and in moments of sorrow and stillness, as if to whisper from the beyond: "I am still here." Their presence is believed to be a sign that the veil has thinned, that our loved ones are near, and that divine love never truly leaves. Some say cardinals appear when angels are near. Others believe they come when comfort is needed the most. I have come to believe each aspect. Feeling and seeing it, to this very day.

In the days following Amanda's passing, a cardinal began crashing into the window, again and again, each time with greater force. It wasn't a gentle tap, but a determined, relentless striking into the glass, as if trying to break through the barrier between here and there. I spoke in silence, "Please stop . . . Are you trying to break your neck?" Words born from the ache of grief and a mother's shattered heart. Now I know. It was you, Amanda. You weren't crashing in distress. You were breaking through. Making your presence known in a language only the soul could understand when graced allows.

Then, one day, the crashing stopped. And something beautiful began. The cardinal returned, sometimes alone, sometimes with its mate, not with urgency, but with calm. Perching just outside my window, she began to sing. Softly at first, then in clear melodic tones, harmonizing with Amanda's favorites, still finding her way home to me, again and again, through every feathered beat, every moment of stillness, and every note.

* * *

Looking back, as vividly as if it were happening this very moment, my pregnancy with you was a battled wrapped in hope. After multiple surgeries to even hold the possibility of conceiving, you came through, spirit becoming flesh.

After eight continuous weeks of hospitalization due to going into preterm labor, Amanda arrived in this world still as a preemie baby by an emergency C-section after doctors discovered that she was in severe fetal distress. Her early days were spent in the neonatal unit until the day that I finally got to bring my miracle home. Those early days and weeks and years were filled with visits to specialists of every kind—renal specialists, otolaryngologists, early child development specialists, physicians of every kind, all focused on helping her thrive through developmental and learning delays.

From the very beginning, and I do mean the beginning, perhaps from conception, her dynamic personality spoke volumes, as it still speaks through me today. I would often find myself smiling and shaking my head, laughing softly within, thinking to myself, *of course, my child is like catching a tiger by the tail.*

It became my sacred calling to be her loving anchor and her ally, believing in her with my whole heart. As she grew, I began to recognize parts of myself within her, especially in the fierce determination that lit her path. Determination without measure, to live her truth, to honor her singular essence, and to bring to life every vision she carried in her heart. Over time, she earned the nickname "DeManda," for when something mattered to her, she stood her ground with unwavering insistence, determined to do things in her own way. She refused to let her flame be dimmed, carrying her heart's desires into being. Through this resolute will, she upheld the vow she made to her own soul and the sacred agreement we made together, ensuring both would be fulfilled exactly as our beings had promised in the time before this life.

"There are no coincidences, only divine appointments."

—Wayne Dyer

Amanda seemed to be leaving me a trail of signs to follow. One of them was the number 22 which she carried on her keychain. Now I understand from my studies that number 22 is known as the architect of dreams. It carries the intuitive insights of number 11 combined with the practical skills of 4. When 22 appears, it signals the soul's ability to bring spiritual vision into material reality."

On 2.2.22 Amanda moved on to her next sacred assignment, leaving her light as my guide.

It began subtly, as signs do—moving into the ordinary, cloaked with grace. I was driving to see my family when the sacred familiar made itself known once again. In front of me, a van came into my view. Its lettering read Amanda's Landscaping Service, and its phone number ended in 2222. I blinked through the cascading tears, causing me to glance down and notice that the arrival time on my GPS was 2:22 p.m. My heart fluttered with that undeniable thrum of recognition, the kind that pulses through when the universe whispers directly to you. In that instant, Adele's "Easy on

Me" began to play, her voice carrying both the ache of letting go and the gentleness of Amanda asking me to understand why she had to go. This song wrapped around me soon after her graduation from Earth, each note an echo of what Amanda might have sung herself. A moment divinely placed, revealing yet another layer of truth in my journey. Another quiet sign from Amanda that she was still here, guiding me with grace, an invitation asking me to soften my heart, to keep believing, while singing to me in ways my heart would fully understand. It felt as if she were whispering to me, gently reminding me: Be easy with your heart, Mama. I'm still with you. I never left you.

> *"The departed do not lose their individual identity or consciousness. They merely shed the physical form and retain their finer mental and emotional natures. They can see and hear us more clearly than before. They even communicate through receptive mediums, or by appearing to loved ones in dreams or visions."*
>
> **—Paramahansa Yogananda**

Some moments feel as if the veil between this world and the next grows thin—when the unseen brushes gently against the seen. It was an ordinary day, in an unremarkable place, when a woman looked at me with a gaze that felt deeper than coincidence. Her voice was calm, steady, filled with knowing. "She says she's sorry. If she had known how much pain her leaving would cause, she would've found another way."

As my mind tried to comprehend what was just said to me, she continued, "It's okay to feel anger, to grieve how things unfolded. But you must forgive—not just her, not yourself, but others."

Then, with quiet reverence, she traced the letter M in the air with her fingers. "There are two presences with 'EMM' sounds in their names that you must forgive." And there were, in fact, two lights in Amanda's life, a girlfriend, the one who held her heart, and her cherished cousin, both with marked by that same echo of the "M" sound. As I looked up with tears rolling down my face, not having spoken a word, it was as though she read my mind. As I thought to myself, *who are you?* She answered somehow knowing what I was thinking. "I am a psychic medium. And Amanda is speaking through me. She is here now."

She spoke gently, not for herself, but as a vessel—bringing Amanda's essence through with clarity and grace. Her presence was unmistakable. Her soul had not died. It had expanded, freed from form, but more present than ever—woven into the very air I breathe, the quiet moments that open the heart, the soft reminders that love is eternal.

* * *

> *"Synchronicity is an ever-present reality for those who have eyes to see it."*
>
> **—Carl Jung**

There are moments when the universe places something before us so striking, so perfectly aligned, that it feels like a whisper from the beyond—a secret reminder that we are not alone and that the ones we love walk beside us still.

On the final healing retreat together, Amanda and I sojourned to Bali, Indonesia—a journey that became a secret closing and an eternal opening.

We immersed ourselves fully into the beauty of the culture: the reverent way the Balinese people honor the divine in every day, the gentle rhythm of their days, the pure kindness extended to us at every turn. We wandered through villages and temples, tasted food infused with ceremony, and danced alongside children under canopies of light and incense.

We visited artisan workshops where hands shaped silver and stones with the patience of generations, and we stepped into art galleries that whispered stories from before time.

In one of those galleries, we came upon a painting—three phases of a ballerina in motion. We stood transfixed, both of us, as we looked up to the figure in the painting that was Amanda. Every detail—her eyes, her lips, the softness of her curls, the posture of her body and flow—was unmistakably hers.

One by one, others in the gallery turned to look at Amanda, then back at the painting, their expressions mirroring our awe. Time paused. Something ancient stirred.

In that moment, we both knew: the image before us was a glimpse of a life she had once lived. She had walked this earth before, danced through time and grace and discipline. Her soul, eternal. Her spirit, never new, only returning.

Now, in retrospect, that moment lives again in me. A gentle reminder that we are all eternal dancers—our steps never lost, our essence never undone.

Through it all, I have come to know this: having the strength to rise is not the absence of struggle—it is the sacred willingness to keep going, even when the path disappears beneath your feet. Every obstacle, every heartbreak, was placed not to punish, but to sculpt, to shape me, to shape all of us into something more true.

Only in the stillness—those quiet moments of breath and reflection—can we begin to see the truth: that change is not only inevitable but imperative to life itself.

We are not merely flesh and bones walking this earth. We are more than atoms and particles serving only a scientific role. We are stardust made conscious, particles luminous and alive, drawn together by divine intelligence to form a bodily vessels through which souls may evolve—across lifetimes, across dimensions, through time and tides.

There is no end to a soul. Souls do not die. They shift, they shimmer, they pass through veils, unseen, carrying with them the wisdom, the beauty, the love of all they have ever touched.

> *"The soul is partly in time and partly in eternity. We are like travelers with a foot in both worlds."*
>
> **—Carl Jung**

Amanda came into this world not only as my daughter, but as my teacher, my soul mirror, my revealer. Her mission was clear: to awaken me. And somehow, mine was to carry her essence into the world—to help fulfill what she began. This isn't just the story of a daughter lost. It is the story of two souls, united in eternity, fulfilling a sacred promise to one another.

My wings are no longer borrowed. They are built in—forged by fire, lifted by grace, and made strong through the love that dared to break me open. They rise with the light of Amanda's spirit guiding me, and with each beat, I soar. I soar with courage. I soar with wisdom. I soar with grace. And above all else, I soar with love.

Now, as I fly in realms higher than those I first knew upon arriving here, I have come to understand that we are not new to this place, only newly awakened to its light. We have worn many faces, walked many roads, loved and lost beneath countless suns and moons. This life is not the first verse of our song, it is simply where the melody returns, carrying with it every note we have ever sung, and every truth we have ever known.

And so I leave you with this knowing: the light Amanda bestowed upon me now burns bright with hope and clarity, not only for my path, but for all of ours.

From where she is, I feel her whispers . . . the signs are just waiting to be discovered. Follow them. And remember, the light burns brightest from its core. Let it be your guide. And when you do, you will rise in the quiet power of your soul, walking with both courage and grace into the life you were meant to live, with certainty that the light within never fades and will always lead you home.

As I set down the last words of my offering, the cardinal appears outside my window, her song in the wind, a song only my soul understands, Amanda reminding me, "I'm right here, Mama."

About Cinzia Marie

Cinzia Marie is a spiritual memoirist, intuitive healer, ceremonialist, and former Senior Court Reporter whose life was forever transformed by the soul contract she shared with her daughter, Amanda. For over 30 years, she served in New York Supreme, Family, and Criminal Courts, bearing witness to the full spectrum of human experience.

After a devastating car accident and multiple surgeries, Cinzia suffered paralysis in her left leg and spent over two years in a wheelchair during the isolating COVID era.

Then, on 2.2.22, her only daughter, Amanda, left her body — a passage that dismantled everything familiar, guiding her toward deeper truths of connection and purpose. In the wake of Amanda's passing, Cinzia immersed herself in expansive inner study-beginning with A Course in Miracles, The Law of One, The Bhagavad Gita, the teachings of Paramahansa Yogananda, Dolores Cannon, sacred feminine wisdoms, and world religions — ultimately arriving at the mystical teachings of Kabbalah. These paths, along with the artistic and soulful wisdom Amanda planted as seeds of remembrance, helped Cinzia transmute grief into purpose and begin holding space for others to reconnect with their light.

Her debut memoir, *You stay . . . I go . . . No following*, is a poetic and powerful journey through eternal love, signs from beyond, and the soul's capacity to rise. With the clarity of ancient truths and the softness of a mother's love, Cinzia now weaves her wisdom and light in healing spaces, retreats, circles, and personal sessions — offering hope, remembrance, and the safety of being truly seen, heard, understood, accepted, and-above all else-loved.

Follow Cinzia on:

Instagram: @beyondsoulga
Email: beyondsoulga@gmail.com
Phone: 646.739.8866

Just Keep Moving

Nicole Smith Levay

Author's Note: This essay was first published in the 2023 anthology Moments That Matter and is republished here with permission. *It began as a private journal entry in 2017, written to help me process and cope during a challenging period. Between 2017 and 2023, with encouragement from friends and colleagues who read early drafts, I revisited and refined the piece many times before it eventually found its way into publication.*

I was four years old when I suffered the trauma that would forever change my life. My family and I were in our golden-beige minivan on our way to my cousin's Christening. There was broccoli salad in a tray lying on the floor between the seats up front. My father was driving, little brother was in a booster seat to my left, and my mother was in front of me. We were going up a winding hill on a rural road in New Jersey.

Then, it happened.

We crashed.

While I was too little to understand what happened or for my memory to store the details for years to come, I do remember, somatically, the moments before impact. The car screeched and spun slightly, the glass window shattered and sprinkled inside the vehicle. I can feel this in my guts, my lower back, as a picture comes to mind: my mother averting her face and lifting her arms. There is broccoli salad in the air. There is no sound and I can't see what happens next.

Many years later, after sorting through various conversations, I uncovered what really happened. The other driver coming down the hill was in our lane, so my father had to make a quick decision: Turn the car off the hill into the trees or turn into the lane the oncoming car was supposed to be in? He chose the latter. He spun the wheel to the left but, in a split second, the other driver corrected his trajectory and moved to the same lane. It was too late to prevent tragedy from happening. The other driver crashed into my door. The impact sent us into the trees.

The next thing I remember is that I'm being cradled in my grandmother's arms. She is running with me toward a house and there is a lot of blood. I am choked for air, unable to make a sound. Eventually it comes, hard and slow, like a roar that shakes my soul. I cry a lot, echoing everybody else's cries as they lay me on a kitchen island. There is a light and I look up. In that moment, both the pain and the memory fade away. After that, only fragments: the ambulance, the hospital, an enormous cast on my right leg, my welcome home party with Cookie Monster.

Then, life went on. There was no talk about it in my conscious memories. For twenty-eight years, nobody spoke about it. Until I could no longer stand the silence. Or, my body began screaming at me, forcing me to break the silence. The expression "the body keeps the score" is true. As I write this for the first time, I can't feel my body. Trauma has a way of residing within you if you never confront and treat it.

What is trauma? How does it affect us and how does it ripple through the rest of our adulthood? Whether consciously or unconsciously, we tend to live our past.

When discussing trauma, I now know we are first and foremost speaking about the nervous system's response to an event, versus an actual event that happened. Trauma is subjective: the body system reacts in a fight, flight, freeze, or fawn state because our electrical current—our nervous system energy—says: "TOO MUCH TOO FAST, MAKE IT STOP!" Then the body and mind come up with clever ways to do exactly that:

1. Fight: lash out and project onto others, literally engage the body in aggression
2. Flight: disassociate or "leave" your body by spacing or numbing out
3. Freeze: breath is held, a shock that lasts long after the initial event
4. Fawn: goes into caretaking others, dismissing one's own needs

Trauma takes on a life of its own. What is overwhelming to the system becomes split off and fragmented into emotions, images, thoughts, and physical sensations that intrude into the present until resolved. How could I possibly assume to know what's right around the corner at all times? Even if my mind told me I couldn't, I felt my body fantasized that it could. Hypervigilance had become my norm.

An armoring in my muscles, tensing within my joints, and a static and charged energy around the perimeter of my body. Aura small, eyes wide, eyebrows lifted. Body bolted by the worries and fears of the pain maybe to come.

Be afraid of what might happen, that'll help just in case, I told myself. *Brace for that impact, from any angle.*

* * *

Even with all that hyper-alertness, the traumatic survival pattern repeated itself. It was as if it was written on me: *let the crisis come to me, I will handle it.* A little girl carrying so much emotional responsibility. Where does the heaviness go when it can no longer be held?

From age five to twenty-two, I danced two to eight hours a day, at least five or six days a week. I had chronic back pain ever since. Even now, after endless treatments and therapy, I experience issues in my spine occasionally. When I first started physical therapy, hunched over like an old woman wincing in pain, people would panic seeing such an unfamiliar site and awkwardly ask: "How could such a young woman hurt her back so badly? It's just not right!" I felt I needed to answer them, but had no idea. Someone did know the answer, *I just didn't know yet.* It wasn't even that I was too young to remember what happened, but I had blacked out during the most significant accident in my life.

At the time of my first bouts of chronic pain I was a young professional dancer, working hard. I blamed myself for a lack of awareness, not enough stretching, bad diet, or something else. Trauma has a way of making us feel like we are not enough and that everything is our fault. It robs us of our inherent lifeforce power, and leaves us riddled in fear, inner conflict, and lack of trust in what we perceive.

Years after repeated injuries, a doctor finally noticed that my right leg was significantly shorter than my left, a bit more than a half of an inch. How did this happen? This was not hip displacement, or caused by stress. The bones were different lengths.

I didn't know what to say when people asked how I hurt myself. I remembered vague mentions of a car accident from family members, along with scattered flashback-like images that hinted at something significant. There had been a settlement check connected to that accident, money that later helped cover both continuing education and life expenses in my late twenties. I had seen photos of myself in a cast, but beyond that, I knew nothing. We didn't talk about it in our house.

Twenty-four years after the car accident, I learned I had a physiological disability I didn't know about. My leg length discrepancy resulted in severe herniations in several vertebrae in my spine because of all of the asymmetric high intensity training through the years, unevenly compressing the discs. This meant a continuation of costly health care bills, and more painfully, I was told by multiple doctors that I would also need to transition out of my dancing career. This idea was traumatizing to my sense of self and my identity. There was also the physical trauma of not being able to walk, regular debilitating spine pain, and blacking out. All of the senses firing DANGER—ears ringing, seeing spots, hallucinations, full body migraines, being so dizzy I felt I could literally leave my body and disappear. I experienced these symptoms regularly. Not to mention the utter endless pain of grief in losing a piece of my soul as a dancer, never to be the same. It is still a daily practice of letting go of a life I embodied that I physically do not and will not have access to (at least in that way) ever again. Going from someone who felt at times like a superhuman athlete of God, spinning in multiple circles up on their toes, jumping six feet in the air, lifting other bodies upon their own, to someone who lives with chronic pain and needs customized orthotics to function, is a messy and frustrating transition.

Dance as a performance profession was perhaps not the exact path I would have followed for myself, as I gradually discovered in the unwinding of my identity. I didn't know what movement therapy was, but since my teenage years, I knew when I'd let my body move freely and turn my brain off, I felt better afterward. I was less mentally off-balance when I'd let my body play off-balance physically. Just letting myself move without any plan or structure, the body leading the way, was healing to me. Whereas dance as performance? I didn't love the perfectionism of rehearsing, nor the moments after shows where people stand around and talk. I was gifted in it though, and once you choose dance performance as your career path beyond high school, it feels like all or nothing. You can't fake it till you make it to become a professional modern dancer in the most cutthroat of all places: New York City. You have to put every ounce of your body, mind, breath, and soul into your training and networking. Every moment is a performance being judged. I had no energy for a backup plan at twenty-eight because I was excelling and feeling confident about my life. I made all my income from what I trained to do my whole life. This was something that happened to dancers in their forties or fifties, I thought. My life felt like it was slipping through my fingers. I didn't know where and when the bottom would hit.

Out of this healing crisis, I moved onto yoga, meditation, and life coaching certifications, and a few years later, I began a master's program in somatic psychology. I also saw a somatic therapist. At the completion of my course studies in trauma, I broached the subject with my therapist and told her that, as a child, I was in a bad car accident and didn't know what happened.

While just talking about the trauma is not helpful by itself and can often just reinstate post-traumatic symptom cycles, being aware of the details of what happened in the event, and working with a trained somatic therapist, can help slow the symptom cycles, untangle them, and repattern in the present moment.

Close to five years after my official career transition from dance performing, I asked to speak with my parents about the accident. On a scheduled meeting, I spoke with my mother on Skype video.

"They said you would most likely grow up to have a physical disability because you broke your growth plate, which is why you got the settlement checks, I guess." She said, shrugging. "That's why they recommended you going into dance classes, for your bone health or something."

Oh, okay. Most likely grow up to have a physical disability?

Well, that was important information about *my* body for me to learn thirty years later! I was completely in shock.

You would most likely grow up to have a physical disability was on a loop in my mind.

* * *

After the conversation, I raged. Angry, big, fat tears, sobbing for that little girl and for the grown woman who ended her dance career far too early. Moments of what felt like anxious insanity bordering on what I know to be a panic attack, and then the crash—deep depression. I texted my husband and told him we couldn't go out that night as I felt broken open. I couldn't remember the last time my nervous system exploded that way. To hold the sadness of multiple versions of myself at once was almost too much.

Before therapy and learning ways to care for myself when in distress, I don't know if I would have survived it. Unintegrated trauma in the body-mind continuum creates chronic hypo- and hyper-arousal of the nervous system. These are states that Western medicine refers to as depression and anxiety.

My thoughts were spinning into paranoia: *What is real? Do I even know my parents? Where is the ground beneath me?* I was in a trauma catharsis vortex. Too much too fast. My brain was a piece of cooked fish, my body had been fileted.

I withdraw more deeply. I didn't know how to feel about this, confused. I was numb. I entered a haze of questioning, though I knew that wouldn't help. The answers often lie in the opposite: in surrendering, releasing, and opening to a power greater than myself.

But I couldn't help it. I had entered that familiar state of analysis and preoccupation. A trauma response roughly 30 percent of Americans know well in their lifetimes, which inevitably is diagnosed as anxiety. I felt like a much younger, less safe version of myself.

Laying on the couch lifeless, I wondered: Did my parents keep this selective omission a secret all these years because they were ashamed that they had been negligent? Or did they think it would be more beneficial to ignore the possibility of pain, taking the all-too-familiar "be positive" approach?

Then I discovered more omissions. From a manila folder of documents *I learned that the person "I" had sued for my "injuries and related lifelong suffering," and the person paying me these settlement checks was, in fact, my own father, the father I love dearly and was a safe space my entire life.* More confusion. How is it that only now, after my initiations, I am learning about all of this?

All these parts within me—empathy, anger, sadness, and intellectual defenses—compete for attention, for someone to hear my version of the story. It's deeply clouded my ability to be in the room, here and now. I'm frozen and dead inside and want to move this energy—yell, scream, cry, shake, something! It feels like too many unspoken stories wanting to live and breathe so badly out in the world, and out of me.

* * *

I see and feel that my parents know they were in over their heads so many times. As a parent myself now, I can understand how sometimes your best just isn't enough. What if my parents were continually making decisions based on their own inherited traumas, lived traumas, and fears caused by their own PTSD?

I am stepping outside my personal pain to acknowledge the weight of intergenerational traumas I have been living out all these years. When things feel unbearable to carry alone it is because it wasn't created alone. We are the stories we have learned, we continue to tell ourselves, and we pass these onto our children in words, actions, and energy.

Perhaps I can be someone to draw a line in the sand in this family, look the beast in the eye and say: no more pretending, the trauma stops here.

* * *

In my therapist's office we somatically worked with the frozen moment of impact after having learned that I was a not-buckled-in child that had flown off the seat. The body does keep the score. *Or rather, my body knew about the accident long before I did.*

This is an abbreviated version of what I went through in my session that I feel I successfully avoided for decades because of lack of information, fear, and unconscious resistance. In slow motion, we recreated where my body had blacked out: I feel my arms covering my face, my legs going limp, the lightness overcoming my body. I take a deep breath and cry. The familiar feeling of numb. Both comforting and erasing. Almost like getting high, but better—no shame involved.

"My body is so smart," I whimper and cry.

I had hated her—my body—for so long for all of this pain and confusion. It's starting to make "sense" what has happened since as a defense to the impact. Lying heavy and stuck now in a lump on my therapist's couch, but feeling that I'm in the car, turning my head, trying to see but can't, my jaw and muscles tensing. I'm hearing the screaming and trembling of my baby brother and my mother who is still in her seat. I want to reach out for my brother but can't; I want to get up but can't. My right leg feels awful.

I don't want to respond to my therapist's prompts. I feel like I'm dead, but too sad to admit it. The good news is, it's really thirty years later, and now I can. My body piecing together this narrative, but then completing the cycle of sensation and activity feels so satisfying to recreate and move the stuck traumatic energy.

"What does your body want to do now?" The therapist says. Slowly.

I want to get up and out of this car, obviously, I think. But I'm there for a long time waiting and waiting for something to shift.

Finally, I slowly start to feel my leg again and the urge to stand sets in. It's like I come back into my body, my back cracks, the little bones in my lower right leg snap, crackle, and pop. A rush of energy, I feel much taller and slowly clearer. The first breath I take in feels like I am being reborn.

"How are you now?" Fuzzy in the background. It takes a while to hear and see the room fully again. Thirty minutes have passed to express and complete what was frozen in one minute. I see my therapist so much more clearly than I ever have before. I want to hug her. But . . . I don't. I'm a little too boundless and I fear if I hugged her, I would turn into a crying baby for . . . forever. That's how deeply held I am feeling. I am relieved, and feel released, at least for now, by this powerful experience. Just one of many different somatic integrations that have kept me moving.

* * *

The goal of embodiment, it is said, is to reunite us with ourselves, bring these parts to the light. Yet, for the person with trauma, this homecoming can be painful and needs its own time to blossom. It may even be an understatement that homecoming through embodiment "can be painful;" it is some of the most difficult work to do, and humans can really be endlessly creative to avoid doing it. There are as many countless subconscious, self-sabotaging ways this happens as there are pains to be avoided. And to those who feel stuck, all over the place, and still ready to do the work, I say have faith. Liberation will eventually occur because the body wants to heal itself; the soul wants to integrate the truth.

Perhaps it helps to consider another perspective: "*Nothing goes away until it has taught us what we need to know.*" – Pema Chödrön.

Years of somatic trauma work have shown me that in recovery, we "choose our hard." We can't hold resentment for the cards we were dealt. Forgiveness is less about excusing the offending party and more about freeing ourselves.

If I had not uncovered and processed the ways unintegrated

trauma was running my life, I would still be struggling—unable to regulate my emotions, stuck in people-pleasing, and losing myself in toxic relationship dynamics. Feeling the feelings and moving through the healing is not "easy," but it is profoundly worth it.

Repressing trauma, by contrast, has been linked to lives marked by disconnection, sickness, and even disease. So I say: take the risk. Express what has been repressed. Stay curious, and watch how life opens and transforms for the better.

As a dancer, I had always connected with movement therapy. I wanted and needed it like water. I had nowhere else to process pain; my parents didn't believe in therapy or God back then, so neither did I for the first half of my life. These two common places people went to seek refuge in crisis situations during my adolescent years, my core organizational system told me wouldn't work or wasn't real. I had few options, so I made my own.

When I improvised, I'd come in contact with these unintegrated fears of impact from the accident. Though they were subconsciously present all the time, in movement therapy they would rise up and take shape. There were shadow forces that would push me over, fling me sideways, or throw me down onto the floor. The gesture of hands coming up to protect my face always surfaced. These were not conscious choices (because at the time I wasn't even conscious of those memories!) but rose from the depths of my unconscious.

When given the chance to partner with another, when all five feet, ten inches of my body would be cradled and walked forward, I'd somatically remember that moment of my grandmother's sprint from the car. Every time. I can still feel the thud-thud-thud of her feet on the ground through my body, and my head resting against her racing heart. Complete surrender and love.

* * *

I am grateful for the tragedies and unique life experiences that I've come through, too. This enables me to help others. I've been able to pay for continuing education thanks to the car accident settlement check. Even before the training, it was like my soul and body knew what to do. It's been bittersweet to look back on my life's journey and see all the roads leading to here. Something was guiding me home.

Our bodies are so smart, and we can learn to access their wisdom and self-healing capacities.

"What do I do now?" I'd ask my body in moments of desperate need, paralyzed by what felt like some unbreakable mental state.

Her answer has always been, "Just keep moving."

I understand now what she was seeking because that's how trauma works. "I" was never stuck, but the memory was. Just keep moving.

Made in the USA
Coppell, TX
15 June 2026

81364216R00085